BEESON
PASTORAL SERIES

BUILDING
TEAMS
IN MINISTRY

DALE GALLOWAY
AND BEESON INSTITUTE COLLEAGUES

Beacon Hill Press of Kansas City
Kansas City, Missouri

Library of Congress Cataloging-in-Publication Data

Galloway, Dale E.
    Building teams in ministry / Dale Galloway and Beeson Institute colleagues.
        p.   cm. — (Beeson pastoral series)
    ISBN 0-8341-1779-7
    1. Lay ministry. 2. Group ministry. I. Title. II. Series.

    BV677.G34 2000
    253—dc21

                                                            00-059894

10   9   8   7   6   5   4   3   2   1

Contents

Acknowledgments

I want to thank each of the contributors to this book. Each is a personal friend who has enriched my life. I have learned much from the ministries of John Ed Mathison, Jim Jackson, Mike Foss, Jim Garlow, and Carl George. I thank God for each of them.

My appreciation also goes to Maxie Dunnam, president of Asbury Theological Seminary, for his vision and support of the Beeson Institute for Advanced Church Leadership, at which these messages were initially delivered. I also have a great support team through Asbury's Beeson Center that includes Barbara Holsinger, Warren Bird, Penny Ruot, Stephanie Hall, Doug Penix, Lori Page, and numerous others, all of whom have advised or helped create the learning contexts that eventually resulted in this book. I always want to acknowledge the support of my dear wife, Margi. Her partnership in life and ministry is irreplaceable.

I also want to honor the memory of Ralph Waldo Beeson, an insurance executive whose bequest has generously funded the Beeson Institute.

Finally, I thank Neil and Bonnie Wiseman for their diligent editing, and the Beacon Hill editorial team including Kelly Gallagher and Bonnie Perry for their commitment to produce this strong, accessible edition of these enduring presentations.

Introduction

This book is about the idea of mobilizing people for ministry especially through the use of teams. The best ministry occurs in team contexts, and the best teams emerge when everyone is working out of spiritual giftedness. *Building Teams in Ministry* will help you do teaming well, both on the lay level and within the church staff.

The following pages offer terrific help from some of the best models and trainers across the country. Their sound advice should add clarity to your journey and reduce the likelihood of missteps. You'll learn how to be more focused as a church and as individuals, all to the glory of the great God we serve.

After learning the concepts contained in this book during my 32 years of pastoring, I sometimes dream of how to put these ideas to work if I had opportunity to pastor again today. I'd approach ministry with two simultaneous strategies, representing the two sections of this book. On the one hand, following section one of this book, I'd be much more intentional about a model where everyone matches his or her gifts and passions to ministry. The following pages show how that's done in many different churches. For example, it's hard to read the Frazer Memorial story (chapter 4) without being amazed at what can happen.

Then on the other hand, I'd again build leaders who build ministries. I'd be even more intentional about small groups as the best places to develop new leaders. This strategy pays great dividends. It's what section two of *Building Teams in Ministry* presents.

I love working with pastors and church leaders, especially when a church has grown to the point of needing leadership from a multistaff team. My prayer is that this collection of insights will add wisdom to your growth as a church, whether you are entering your first multistaff stages or whether you are a veteran in multistaff settings.

Building Teams in Ministry originated through the Beeson Institute for Advanced Church Leadership, a conference that meets at various teaching churches and retreat centers. It is designed as a field-based coaching relationship that accelerates the gift development of senior pastors who want to grow strong, healthy, and effective churches. For more information, such as an introductory video or brochure, contact 888-5BEESON or 859-858-2307, fax 859-858-2274, E-mail <Beeson_Institute@asburyseminary.edu>, or visit <www.asburyseminary.edu> and follow the site index map listing to the Beeson Institute.

This book is part of the ongoing Beeson Pastoral Series designed to help develop you so that you can in turn develop others to their maximum in ministry. Previously published volumes include *Leading with Vision* and *Making Church Relevant*.

SECTION I

Multiply Ministry Through Lay Ministers

▪ 1 ▪

SHARING MINISTRY TOGETHER THROUGH TEAMS
How to Start a Lay Revolution

Dale E. Galloway

*R*evolution—that explosive word jumped off the page of a book I was reading in the early days of my ministry. The sentence surrounding that word *revolution* changed my concept of ministry forever. "If the average church should suddenly take seriously the notion that every lay member—man or woman—is really a minister of Christ, we could have something like a *revolution* in a very short time." That new insight was proposed by Elton Trueblood—beloved teacher, influential thinker, Quaker writer, and founder of the Yokefellows.

Trueblood reinforced his idea in another epic sentence that stretches me to this day: "The laity are not the passengers of a ship, but members of the crew." After encountering Trueblood's ideas, I started thinking how to maximize the potential of lay ministries in the development of a new church I started in Portland, Oregon.

As I pondered the potential of lay ministry, I saw shared ministry as an effective way to multiply the work of God. The possibilities are fantastic, almost unbelievable. When laypeople and pastor join together in meaningful ministry, the church thrives and develops spiritually.

Nearly everything God calls a church to do can be achieved with increased effectiveness through lay involvement in small groups. That includes a long list of desirable accomplishments like service, accountability, spiritual friendship, acceptance, Bible study, pastoral care, and learning better how to apply faith to

When mutual ministry is emphasized and a system of shared ministry is developed, an amazing multiplication takes many forms.

life. When mutual ministry is emphasized and a system of shared ministry is developed, an amazing multiplication takes many forms—all of them significant. More persons are won to Christ. More believers are nurtured in the faith. More service satisfaction is experienced by more believers. Healthy churches result. As we know, a kind of synergism of strength happens when a team of horses pull together: one can pull a full load, but two working together can pull the weight of five or six loads. Lay ministry is like that. It multiplies mission achievement for any church. It applies increased energy that helps make dreams and visions become realities.

Consider the explosive growth of the Church and the redemptive impact on society if every Christian had a significant part in achieving Christ's mission through the Church in the world. Imagine how such a trajectory of mobilizing laypeople could stimulate the awakening that is so desperately needed.

OVERCOMING POPULAR MYTHS

Miraculous seeds for renewal and Kingdom expansion wait to be planted through lay ministry. However, several myths limit our vision concerning lay ministry. By myths I mean widely held misconceptions that have been repeated over decades and generations without close scrutiny. Having heard them so frequently, we accept them as true. Take a hard look at these mirages that are often seen on the horizons of ministry.

• **There are two classes of Christians, clergy and laity.** Scripture gives no support to this mistaken idea, even though it is commonly accepted in Western society. This notion apparently started as early as A.D. 325 in the Council of Nicaea. The reality— the Church has no second-class citizens, according to Scripture.

• **The clergy give ministry; the laity receive ministry.** Thoughtful study of the New Testament shows it is nearly impossible to identify differences between laity and clergy in their service for Christ in the Early Church. The Gospels and Epistles call for every believer's full participation and provide no place for spectator religion. Everyone participated on the playing field. No one watched from the sidelines. Near the dawn of Christianity, being a follower of Jesus meant serious, all-out commitment to His ambitious plans to impact the world. Every Christian was expected and equipped to give as well as receive ministry.

In the Church's present state, many laity are overstuffed with preaching and saturated with teaching. Many pastors, at the same time, feel famished from giving so much so often. No coach, however talented, could win a game if the team members are seated in the stands.

• **A person becomes a minister by formal education and ordination.** George Hunter tells us how it was at the dawn of the Christian era: "Neither Jesus, nor any of the apostles, nor any one else was 'ordained' in the sense now meant by any denominational tradition today. The followers of Jesus, according to their gifts, ministered to each other and to other people, and they penetrated the Mediterranean world as the salt of the earth, the light of the world, and as those who 'turned the world upside down.'" Action to meet needs was the way they authenticated their ministry and strengthened their faith.

• **Trained clergy are more effective than laypeople.** Though the Body of Christ requires trained clergy to lead and equip others for service, every believer can do some form of ministry and do it well. Two irrefutable principles of church history can be seen at work in churches across the world today: (1) The church stagnates or declines when clergy hoard ministry as their elite possession. (2) The church thrives and transforms new believers when ministry is shared with laypeople.

• **Lay ministry is something that just happens.** Everything lasting and significant the Church accomplishes must be intentional. It must have purposeful planning, effective promotion, careful training, and persistent implementation. Starting a lay ministry revolution in your setting cannot be achieved without your creative instruction, positive support, and resolute willingness to share responsibility. Issues of authority and credit must be faced squarely and shared willingly.

These myths are exactly that—myths. For lay ministry to be accepted and effective, each of these inaccurate perceptions must be lovingly challenged and thoughtfully corrected.

Change that encourages lay ministry almost never comes from pulpit pronouncements alone. *Oughts* and *shoulds* won't do it. More sermons on duty intended to produce guilt won't accomplish the desired goal either. But a revolution that can result in another spiritual awakening can start from a positive, understandable, well-constructed plan for meaningful lay opportunities for ministry. And it can start in your church.

In her book *Jesus CEO*, Laurie Beth Jones plainly explains the benefits: "Jesus clearly and consistently conveyed to his staff the significance of what they were doing. He spoke long and often about the calling, and they could feel and see the long-lasting benefits of their work with him. They were changing people's lives for the good" (178-79). Conveying significance and sharing of satisfaction are among the most important keys to motivating laypersons for ministry. No one serves for long without some sense of fulfillment. The Psalmist's song is true: "Serve the LORD with gladness; come before Him with joyful singing" (100:2, NASB). Every believer must be helped to understand that doing ministry brings incredible joy to those who serve fully as much as it helps those who are served.

CUTTING-EDGE CHURCHES JUMP-START THIS NEW REFORMATION

Note how quickly a revolutionary concept of lay ministry turns into a reformation. Recovering a Bible ideal does that. First the idea moves from resistance to change to an implementation that produces a quantum leap forward for a church. Veteran pastor Melvin J. Steinbron, in his helpful book *The Lay-Driven Church,* strongly believes the lay ministry movement is a second reformation. So do I. He writes, "In the first reformation, the church gave the Bible to the people. In the second reformation, the church gave ministry to the people." Should this second reformation have as much impact as the first, a great spiritual awakening would likely reach into every cranny of Western civilization.

When such a reformation of lay ministry starts in a congregation, the church thrives. Then that church becomes a high-impact congregation. It becomes an instrument God uses to transform lives, accomplish astounding achievements, and challenge other congregations across the land to move to the front lines of battle and service.

Lay Ministry More than a Fad

Please note that this reformation is not a passing fad that works only in a few places. Rather, it results from a rediscovery of the Bible teaching that every Christian is a minister. It recovers Luther's priesthood of all believers. It renews Wesley's practices built into the fabric of the 18th-century Methodist movement when almost all ministry was done by laity. Methodism's unprecedented expansion in Great Britain and America resulted from the laity fulfilling the mission of Christ in their world. The fact is inescapable—lay ministry was a reproducible ingredient of the Wesleyan revival. Wesley's rediscovery of lay ministry left us an impressive legacy.

In visiting churches across America and even outside the United States, I have never visited or heard about a cutting-edge church where laity and clergy do not come close together in mutual ministry. These churches put into practice the biblical principle that every believer is a minister. These congregations place great value on doing ministry together. They embrace Jesus' pattern for multiplying ministry when He equipped a small group of rough fishermen, youthful troublemakers, and hated tax collectors to do ministry in His name. Their credentials were Jesus' directive to "go" (see Acts 1:8.). Their message was the simple, life-transforming gospel (see Luke 24:46-48).

Biblical Pattern Replicated

Contemporary cutting-edge churches seek to replicate our Lord's pattern of building a ministry team. Laurie Beth Jones underscores the importance of such a team: "The truth is that good ideas, noble intentions, brilliant inventions, and miraculous discoveries go nowhere unless somebody forms a team to act on them. Whoever forms a team to carry out the best ideas wins" (*Jesus CEO*, 91). Interesting, isn't it, that Jesus modeled the strength of teaming many centuries before modern managers were even born.

Jesus provides us an amazing model for developing lay ministries. He showed us the values of full participation. He demonstrated that mission cannot be accomplished without a team. In His ministry, it was often a weak, frightened team, but a team no less. In fact, God never gave anyone I have ever heard of a vision for His Church that could be accomplished by the leader alone. A Kingdom vision always requires getting many people involved to transform a dream into reality. Apparently God's way of building His kingdom is to give a leader such a gigantic vision that he or she has to recruit many helpers.

Foundation: Understanding of Ministry

To recruit people for dream achievement requires that a leader have a clear-cut understanding of ministry. That's the basic soil for Kingdom planting and harvesting. Ask yourself, What is ministry? Make your answer specific. And relate your response to your present assignment. Much modern ministry is stalled by a muddled mission.

For me, ministry is some special service done for God. To make that happen, every aspect of ministry must be built on three biblical mountain peaks: the Great Commission, the Great Commandment, and the Great Charge.

You remember that Rick Warren's insightful book *The Purpose-Driven Church* insists that a twin all-out commitment to the Great Commandment and Great Commission will grow a great church. I agree wholeheartedly, and I rejoice that his ideas are shaping congregations around the world.

But I want to add another component that I first heard Melvin Steinbron suggest. To the two peaks of the Great Commission and the Great Commandment, he calls for a wholehearted commitment to the Great Charge. The Great Charge says: "Tend the flock of God that is your charge, not by constraint but willingly, not for shameful gain but eagerly, not as domineering over those in your charge but being examples to the flock" (1 Pet. 5:2-3, RSV). Be an example to the flock—what an authenticating requirement.

Here's a picture of how it works. Fulfilling the Great Charge means a pastor must give wholehearted encouragement, freedom, and space for laypersons to do meaningful ministry. The pastor must sound a frequent call for response. These churches find a place for everyone to minister, and the pastor models shared ministry.

Here's a summary formula for a congregation to implement or increase its effectiveness in lay ministry: thorough commitments to the Great Commission, Great Commandment, and Great Charge.

WHO IS CAPABLE OF DOING MINISTRY?

The answer to that question is all Christians who are serious about their faith and solid in their commitments to Jesus Christ. While no one can do everything, everyone can do something.

To fully consider the implications of lay ministry, pastors must ask and answer these defining questions:

1. How much education is needed to do ministry?
2. What spiritual gifts does one need to do ministry?
3. What do pastors do that laypeople cannot do?
4. What is it that laypeople do that pastors are not good at doing?
5. Who is the closest to where laypeople live and how they think?

The main question concerning the lay ministry issue is, What do pastors do that laypeople cannot do? Carefully think through what you believe about that issue. Your response determines how much you are willing to release laypeople and how you will mobilize them.

We discovered at New Hope Community Church, though it was hard to admit at first, that persons who came up through the lay ministry program were often closer to where people lived than any of the staff. They better understood what common folks thought about life and faith. For these reasons, we learned lay pastors could effectively deal with issues ordinary folks face every day.

Three simple but significant ideas must be carefully built into the foundations of any lay ministry effort:

- Ministry is done in relationships more than in church buildings.
- Shepherds do not produce sheep; sheep produce other sheep.

• Ministry in its purest form is doing love.

I strongly suggest you write those three pivotal concepts near the front of your calendar planner. Post them so they flash across your computer screen saver. Jot them on stick-on notes near your phone. You might even copy them on a front page of your Bible—or memorize them. Keep working with those basic ideas about ministry until they seep into the fabric of your philosophy of ministry. Keep them before you until they become as much a part of how you do ministry as simple math is to balancing your checkbook.

Requirements for Lay Service

Then to set guidelines for lay service, determine the absolutely essential characteristics. These requirements should be biblical, brief, and easy to understand. Here's my list, which you may wish to use in developing your own requirements:

1. Conversion—An authentic relationship with Jesus Christ is absolutely essential. Though lay ministers need not be long-term Christians, they must have a vital relationship to Jesus.

2. Scripture—They must believe the Bible to be the Word of God.

3. Gifts—They must be willing to be taught how to discover and use their ministry gifts.

4. Testimony—In their own way, they must be able to express love for God, the church, and the people they serve.

5. Loyalty—A sense of loyalty to pastor and staff is a plus, though a strong case can be made that these loyalties develop best as laypersons share ministry with clergy leaders.

Though your list should be short, it is absolutely necessary. Should a potential lay minister not have the needed characteristics, a pastor must view as a priority helping that person develop these characteristics so he or she is qualified to do ministry for Christ. The ideal is to help that one become ready rather than to reject the person.

Give special emphasis to the love quotient between yourself, the professional paid staff, and other persons in lay ministry. Church growth specialist Win Arn underlines a New Testament essential when he observed, "Ministry in its purest and simplest form is love. Ministry is, in fact, doing love!" That sounds a lot like Jesus' words, "As I have loved you, so you must love one another. By this all men will know that you are my disciples, if you love one another" (John 13:34-35).

Every expression of ministry must be saturated with the love of Christ—fully understood by those who serve. E. Stanley Jones in *The Reconstruction of the Church—On What Pattern?* beautifully explains the idea: "The church, when it is the real church, is a society of organized love. It teaches young and old to live together as members of a society that cares, cares for everybody everywhere" (25).

To Institute Lay Ministry, Pastors Must Change

The pastor must first change perspective and practice before lay ministry can flourish. Such a change may be difficult because so many ministers have for years been steeped by their preparation and practice to believe real ministry has to be done by them. In this concept, laypersons were welcome to assist, but the ordained head of the church was the one who did real ministry.

Change Even When a Church Is Growing

One of the hardest lessons for me to learn in my journey of growing a church from zero to several thousand was that I had to change before the church changed. Across the years in Portland at every level of growth, I had to change before we could move to the next level. James C. Fenhagen explains the reasons in his book *Mutual Ministry:* "The pastor, for good or for ill, is in a position to encourage and support or to block and dilute whatever initiative emerges in the congregation at large. When he or she is inept or depressed, the life of the entire congregation is affected. When he or she is excited about what is going on, and *is growing inwardly and acquiring new skills* [italics mine], the congregation is generally the primary beneficiary" (113).

Growing is hard work for those like me who find it hard to change. For the pastor, change is especially hard when the church is growing and new converts are being won. That's when it is easy to believe everything you are doing and thinking is what makes the church grow.

A pastor I know has succeeded so well at big event evangelism that he has a great crowd every Sunday morning. He reasons that since his church has increased attendance, he sees no reason to put a pastoral care strategy and an assimilation system in place. As a result, he has a crowd but not a church. He is victimized by his own effectiveness. He does not understand the necessity of changing himself before the church can change. He excuses himself from personal growth for the next phase of his church's development by saying, "Look how well what we are doing is working."

> *Most organizations don't change*
> *until they have to.*
> *—Robert Kriegel*

When some of his best people moved to other churches, he made himself believe they did not want new people, when in fact they desired a growing *church* instead of a crowd of strangers. The church he serves will never be healthy and balanced until he sees a need to change himself. And his conclusions about some of his best people are absolutely false.

In his stimulating management book *If It Ain't Broke . . . Break It!* Robert Kriegel offers advice to business leaders that also provides a serious caution for clergy: "Most organizations don't change until they have to. They wait until things are going poorly and then desperately try to find a quick fix, changing strategies, products, services—anything to try to catch up. The problem is that you don't think clearly with a gun at your head. The poor decision making, lack of innovation, and low morale characteristic of organizations playing catch-up create a vicious cycle that keeps them significantly behind" (76). Before a church changes, its pastor must change.

What Pastors Have to Give Up to Implement Lay Ministry

Several tricky issues must be faced if a pastor wants to build authentic, effective lay ministry in his or her church. Some of these concerns are painfully deceptive. That's why they require a deliberate look inside ourselves.

• **Being a hero.** The soloist gets the credit if something sounds especially good in a one-person band. If all goes well in a congregation where the pastor is the solo minister, he or she gets the credit. The limelight is a great feeling, easy to enjoy. But when teams do ministry, there are no heroes—just members of a winning team. After years of solo ministry, beginning to work with and through a team can be extremely difficult for a pastor.

• **Elite status.** Of course, we love the affirmation when members place us on a pedestal. Our egos swell when parishioners gush, "No one does ministry as well as our pastor." Everyone likes to be told they are special and supertalented. But these delightful comments can become a millstone. To believe you deserve elite status is to buy your eventual downfall. In a team ministry, elite status usually goes down to almost zero.

• **Enjoyable ministry.** Satisfaction for pastors often comes from doing those parts of ministry they most enjoy. But lay ministry forces a minister to rethink this issue. So we must ask ourselves whether we are willing to allow others to do phases of ministry we enjoy. Sometimes the things we enjoy most are the things we are most skilled at doing because we have given much energy to developing them. But since we were able to develop this skill, others may well learn it also.

Sometimes the issue is that we know we can do a particular phase better than anyone else in the congregation. This dynamic is like the first time you allow your child to wash the car; you sometimes wish you had done it yourself!

• **Sharing pastoral care.** Perhaps the most satisfying connection between a minister and a parishioner comes in providing pastoral care during times of crises. Pastoral care builds bonds between pastor and parishioner. It also helps inform a pastor's preaching, and it keeps the pastor's heart tender toward human needs.

Nonetheless, pastoral care has to be shared if a church is to grow and if the laity are to develop similar bonds with those they serve. I believe the balance comes from helping others learn how to do pastoral care and allowing them to do it but to never completely give up on doing some pastoral care yourself.

• **The center of attention.** Many pastors stand at the center of everything in the church and are unwilling to move. Leading from the center is natural, or perhaps necessary, especially in a growing church where the pastor was the only leader. When we started New Hope Church in Portland, we had only five or six people. I was the center of everything. I knew everybody. I knew their personalities. I was in their homes. I knew what to expect from them and they from me. But as the church grew, I had to be willing to delegate responsibilities because so much was happening.

Often without fully realizing its effect, the pastor's attitude toward church life is one of keeping a tight rein and controlling everything. Such a practice undermines ministry. This attitude may be the single most limiting growth factor in thousands of small and midsized churches. Often these same pastors think their church does not grow because the congregation does not work hard enough, does not give enough, or is not friendly enough. The real problem, however, is the pastor's unwillingness to give up being at the center and controlling everything that happens in that church.

Equipping Others for Works of Service

If you are not helping laity use their spiritual gifts, you are robbing them of the joy of service. You are not accomplishing the assignment given pastors in Eph. 4:11-13: "It was he [Christ] who gave some to be apostles, some to be prophets, some to be evangelists, and some to be pastors and teachers, to prepare God's people for works of service, so that the body of Christ may be built up until we all reach unity in the faith and in the knowledge of the Son of God and become mature, attaining to the whole measure of the fullness of Christ." That's a pretty amazing summary of what God wants His people to be and do. Though this nurturing/discipling synopsis of ministry has several facets that need thoughtful exegesis, at its basic minimum this passage means pastors have a duty to equip laypeople to do their ministry so the Body of Christ may be healthy and effective.

This passage, however, needs to be preached with one important caution. Every pastor who bases ministry on this passage must not teach or imply that the minister no longer does ministry. In any field, including ministry, trainers are always suspect by followers if they are not practitioners. The old adage is exactly right for a pastor: "Do as I do as well as do as I say." The biblical ideal is to be a player-coach. I believe the passage calls pastors to do ministry alongside laypeople as part of providing training for them to serve effectively.

PRACTICAL WAYS TO ENCOURAGE LAY MINISTRY

1. Communicate vision. The vision God gives you is too big to be accomplished by a few persons. Keep sharing the vision with everyone who will listen, and keep emphasizing how many people are needed and wanted.

2. Require professional staff to be recruiters. No church has enough resources to hire enough people to do all the ministry that is needed. In Portland, we had 18 pastors on the staff, and though each one had some specific specialty and carefully described duties, each job description placed a No. 1 priority on development of lay ministry. Recruiting, motivating, equipping, and involving laypersons in ministry was part of every staff pastor's assignment.

3. Be realistic about time and money limitations. All money does is free people to have more time to do ministry. The motive for ministry must always be higher than money. This is the reason I try not to speak of "hiring" staff members. In an ultimate sense, you cannot pay someone to do ministry.

4. Emphasize spiritual gifts. The Creator gave every person some ministry gift. The church and her leaders must help every congregant discover their gifts and learn how to use those gifts. Value all the ministry gifts as blessings God has bestowed on your congregation.

5. Share satisfactions. Serving people are happy people. The more people become involved in ministry, the higher their level of satisfaction. I love John Ed Mathison's quote: "[People] can't row and rock the boat at the same time."

6. Cultivate esteem from ministry. Just as your self-worth increases when you do ministry, similar positive feelings are experienced by lay ministers. So when we help build a person's ministry, they will build the church. Go back to the Bible and check the Jethro principle. People experience increased self-worth when they are effectively employed in the work of God that is helping change the world. To be an effective, involved child of God produces positive self-worth for every believer.

7. Everyone has a ministry. God charges pastors and congregations with helping folks discover their gifts. He expects the church to employ those gifts efficiently so the church continually reaps the benefits of the combined gift mix. God provided gifts for a specific congregation years before group members even knew each other.

True shepherds never get away from the desire to be involved with the people God entrusts to them.

8. Be realistic about your pastoral care span. If your span of pastoral care is more than 10 persons, you may have limited your ability to lead your church. Yet we have traditionally been taught that a pastor is to personally provide pastoral care. The larger the church, the more difficult this requirement becomes. But pastoral care cannot be abandoned just because the congregation grows too large or because such care is too hard or time-consuming. Never forget these powerful words of Scripture: "They . . . will answer, 'Lord, when did we see you hungry or thirsty or a stranger or needing clothes or sick or in prison, and did not help you?' He will reply, 'I tell you the truth, whatever you did not do for one of the least of these, you did not do for me'" (Matt. 25:44-45).

Pastoral care, a biblical expectation and a human need, cannot be abandoned. The true shepherds never get away from the desire to be involved with the people God entrusts to them. But pastoral care can be effectively shared with laity. Your church has many wonderful caregivers who will do this ministry well after they are given basic training. Pastoral care has to be done, but it does not all have to be done by the senior minister.

9. Model ministry while teaching ministry. Effective lay ministry instruction is not just telling people, but showing them. The model/mentoring approach is an enjoyable way to teach and an effective way to learn.

10. Intentionally develop lay ministry. Such ministry takes place in a church only when it is intentionally planned and thoughtfully implemented. No layperson is likely to even consider becoming involved unless the pastor gets the vision, shares the potential, and ties the whole effort to what Scripture teaches about service. It must be planned, promoted, supported by Scripture, and shown to add value to the one who serves as well as the one served.

All of this is vastly different from the secular delegated leadership model. In the secular business pattern, the leader keeps developing key persons and giving them more responsibility while moving farther and farther away from where the common people are. But to be an authentic servant-leader, ministers must model ministry with a few people around them. This means there will never be a time when the pastor moves completely away from any phase of ministry while everyone else does the work. Rather, as leader, the pastor models what is taught.

E. Stanley Jones in *The Reconstruction of the Church* explains why: "If the laity lead, they will produce leaders. . . . If the church is pastor-centered, then the output will be rhetoric; if it is lay-centered, the output will be action. And there will be meaningful discussion around the action. It will be the Word become flesh instead of the Word become word" (109). What an inspiring idea and what revolutionary action! That's what shared ministry does.

▪2▪

EMPOWERING LEADERS FOR MINISTRY
Leading Change for Increased Effectiveness

Michael W. Foss

Fact, or at least a strong suspicion—85 to 90 percent of Protestant churches are failing across the United States. The way most pastors were trained to do ministry will not take us effectively into the future. Pastors need to rethink purpose and expectations. Doing traditional pastoring ourselves is considerably less effective than equipping others to do it. That takes a critical shift in the thinking and commitments of a pastor.

PASTOR AS PROFESSIONAL

The idea of "pastor as professional" goes back to an older time when the minister was the village intellectual. The people came to him for goodies like baptism, Communion, weddings, and funerals. Sometimes they even asked for a bit of advice. This model worked because the clergy were the best-educated persons in the community and village life centered around the church. Then the parson was somebody important.

At Prince of Peace Lutheran Church where I serve, the "pastor as professional" would not work. All secretaries in the church office have bachelor's degrees. Many church members have master's degrees, and some have Ph.D.'s.

The "pastor as professional" patter was revved in the '50s with what I call the *golden age* of the Protestant church—post-World War II era. That was the old game, and we won it. We planted churches across the country, and the people came. The "pastor as professional" meant sitting in our offices and waiting for people to come to us to dispense counseling and care.

PASTOR AS CHAPLAIN

The mid '60s ushered in the idea of "pastor as chaplain." Many of us say, "I didn't get into that 'pastor as professional' idea, but my mind-set is 'pastor as chaplain.' My job was to make sure the families in my congregation knew me and I knew them. If they had any difficulty, I would be there, in their homes and at their hospital bedsides." Most of us are still living in and servant to that expectation.

If the chaplain model is followed, your congregation is automatically limited to a cap of about 200 in worship attendance. Should you grow beyond that cap, you will be continually stressed by a heavy workload. Few pastors, however gifted, can serve as an effective chaplain to more than 200 people.

The congregation I served in 1982 had 125 in worship when I arrived and grew to more than 450. One Sunday, I experienced a pastoral panic attack when I looked out on the congregation and realized I did not know many of them and I had never been in many of their homes. Only with great effort did I get through my sermon that morning. Neither did it help that my associate knew many I did not know, and I feared they liked him better than me.

I went home to fret and pray. And I heard God tell me, "What right do you have to limit My ministry in this place?"

I was convicted and frightened. So I went to the church council and said, "I have to learn to do ministry differently." I told them I could no longer be everyone's counselor. This sounded to them like a radical idea. Secular psychologists, psychiatrists, and M.D.'s had been referring people to me. I had graduate studies in counseling and was effective at helping people with emotional difficulties. Now I was telling the council, many of whom I had ministered to in counseling, that I could not do it anymore.

They voted unanimously after an hour and a half to release me from that obligation. The president of the council turned to me after the vote and said, "But, of course, that doesn't mean my family and me."

PASTOR AS SPIRITUAL DIRECTOR OR SHEPHERD

What I learned then is that pastors can no longer be visiting caregivers. The only way to do ministry now is to shift to the biblical model of spiritual director or shepherd. The shepherding I have in mind is not what we used to see in the western United States—the shepherd always driving the sheep from behind the flock. No, for our time the pastor-shepherd has to be out in front as a spiritual leader.

I saw an example in Israel on the road to Bethlehem. An old shepherd was walking in front of the flock. Behind him were two rows of animals—one goats and one sheep. The flock followed though taxis, buses, and cars whizzed by. They trusted the shepherd to lead them to where they could be cared for.

In this new millennium, my job is to care about equipping the leaders to equip others to be engaged in ministry. If we are going to set loose the people of God, we must begin to understand that there are laypeople who pray and counsel as well or better than we do. It is all about gifts, not position. It is also about relationships.

A Clarifying Hospital Call

I remember clearly an incident that happened while I was pastor in Beaverton, Oregon. I received a phone call late in the evening informing me that a key lay leader named Marsha was having surgery the next morning.

So I got up at about 5:15, showered to get awake, put on my clerical collar, and drove down the hill into Portland. I went into the hospital and found out her room number.

As I neared her room, a laywoman from our church came out, a member of a small prayer group to which Marsha belonged. She greeted me, "Well, Pastor Mike, what are you doing here?"

I thought, "What do you mean? This is my job. I am supposed to be here. What are *you* doing here?" Instead I gave a more acceptable answer, "Well, I came to see Marsha."

She said, "She's in the room here. We didn't expect you to come."

So I walked in while the lay visitor waited at the doorway. As I entered the room, I observed an inspiring picture of compassion. Another friend, Diane, was sitting on the bed holding Marsha's hand to calm her. Then I realized that all three were in the same prayer group.

As I entered the hospital room, I said, "Hi, Diane. Hi, Marsha." Diane moved out of my way, which was what I thought she should do. As I started talking to Marsha, those two wonderful women of God left so their pastor could do the real job.

I protested, "No, no, no, come on back in. We'll pray together." They reluctantly came back into the room.

Soon after that I left. I was angry as I talked out loud to God about this troubling situation. My inside communication with God heard, "Mike, what are you doing?"

"What do You mean, what am I doing? I'm going back to the office."

"But what have you done?"

"What do You mean, what have I done? I just did my job!"

"Do you think I listen to Diane's prayers less than yours?"

I went back to the office and just sat there and thought, "Lord God, You have to show me what I have to do."

I prayed, "Lord, the pastor as chaplain or the pastor as professional is not working so well. Equip me so that I can be a shepherd of Your people, and help me know how to do it."

More than the Cisco Kid

God's answer required changes that may be difficult for others to accept. Misunderstanding may happen when you try to implement lay ministry in your congregation. Someone will probably tell you the work you want laity to share is your job. Though criticisms come, you must keep developing new strategies of how to serve more people more effectively. Lay ministry, when done effectively, makes all other phases of ministry more available and more effective.

Think for a moment about the Cisco Kid and Pancho or the Lone Ranger and Tonto. Week after week, the community could not solve its own problems, so one of these teams would ride in, take care of the situation in a half hour, and ride away. Most of us in ministry believe that is our job—ride into the family or the church, fix things, and ride off.

When the church grows enough, I can bring in a partner to

play Pancho to my role as Cisco; we would together get it all done.

inistry is about teaming,
and it is a lot less lonely.

It does not work that way anymore. Perhaps we should think as if we are being called to be more like basketball great Phil Jackson. Why did Michael Jordan say that if Phil Jackson was not coming back, "I'm not coming to play"? The reason—Phil Jackson helped Michael Jordan be better than he could have been by himself. And Jordan helped Scotty Pippin be more. Together they helped each other learn to shine in basketball. That is what God is calling you and me to do—help others learn to shine in team ministry.

Michael Jordan played with the Chicago Bulls seven years before they won a playoff game. One of the world's greatest athletes could not win by himself until they brought in other players who could relieve him, feed him, and take his feeds. That is what ministry is about. It is teaming, and it is a lot less lonely. When we shift from the Lone Ranger—get in and fix it and get out—we become part of a community. We do not do it by ourselves.

All the People of God Doing Ministry

This teaming for ministry means, then, that we see the team as more than a church staff—it is all the people of God doing ministry. Think about it this way. How many people in your congregations have five different jobs? If that happens at Prince of Peace Church, I say to our people, "When you hold five jobs, you exclude four other people from ministry."

When put into operation, the replication principle creates new interest, spreads leadership, and keeps existing leaders sensitive to how they are perceived by the group. It significantly cuts a sense of lifelong ownership of a position or task. And it connects the new people with old-timers.

Teaming for the new millennium ministry also requires that we celebrate our inadequacies. As believers we do not have to be adequate or perfect or strong. Somewhere I read that the Church of Jesus Christ is like a spastic person, so we have a perfect Head—Jesus Christ the Lord—who directs His Church, but the hands and feet cannot follow the directives that come from the Head. Though the Head is right, the performance of the body leaves much to be desired.

These concepts remind me of Paul's words: "[Christ] said to me, 'My grace is sufficient for you, for my power is made perfect in weakness.' Therefore I will boast all the more gladly about my weaknesses, so that Christ's power may rest on me" (2 Cor. 12:9).

Every Believer Is Inadequate

One of the best gifts to give your church is to remind them that every believer is inadequate. And though we are inadequate, God provides someone to fill in the gap. I want to challenge you to face your inadequacies. Identify a big need in yourself or in your congregation and begin to pray, "God, help me recognize the person You are calling to meet this need." They will be there.

For example, I cannot play the piano, but I work with a colleague called Handt Hanson who can. I have much bigger hands than his, but that does not make me a pianist. When he sits down at the piano, oh, how he can play!

Our church has a lay member who is a former national strategic planner for U.S. West. When we get together, he knows how to translate dreams, visions, and prayers into strategic plans with clear goals and objectives. He makes many of my ideas happen.

The excellent secular magazine *Fast Company* offered their version of the *Make Yourself a Leader* kit—it is a team approach to grassroots leadership. The new spin emphasizes the need for leaders at all levels of the organization rather than the top-down approach. Unlike the "leader [pastor] has all the answers" model, it focuses on the need for listening and learning and emphasizes the critical pieces about networking with other leaders in order to create more leaders. I highly recommend the kit's 12 easy instructions:

1. Leaders are both confident and modest.
2. Leaders are authentic.
3. Leaders are listeners.

4. Leaders are good at giving encouragement, and they're never satisfied.
5. Leaders provide direction.
6. Leaders make unexpected connections.
7. Leaders protect their people from danger—and expose them to danger.
8. Leaders make change—and stand for values that don't change.
9. Leaders lead by example.
10. Leaders don't blame—they learn.
11. Leaders look for and network with other leaders.
12. The job of the leader: make more leaders.

Committees vs. Ministry Teams

In my first months at Prince of Peace, I was advised that our church constitution needed to be rewritten. This was not exactly music to my ears, but I listened anyway. At that time, council meetings were lasting three hours—not because they were getting things done, but because the 20-plus council members spent their time redoing and undoing what committees under them had already done. Who wants to sit on a committee to do work only to have it reported to a higher body for rethinking? No wonder we could not get people to serve.

We now have three constitutional ministry teams and a multitude of active and interactive ministry teams that never meet longer than 90 minutes—including Bible study. We are fighting to get through the business, and we are centered in the Word of God.

Isn't it interesting that we ask the wonderful people who come and serve the church for spiritual reasons to set those needs aside during meetings for the sake of business? We tip our hat at the Savior by having a five-minute devotional and a quick or closing prayer. And we pretend that it is lay ministry because we ask one of them to do it. At Prince of Peace council meetings, I now lead a 15- to 20-minute Bible study, and the meetings are finished in an hour and a half. If we need to accomplish more business, we call a special meeting.

I certainly do not claim to know all there is to know about the business of the church, but I do understand the importance of church business. I can talk about the business of the church, even though my job is mainly spiritual. I also will not deny my congregation or lay leadership the right to exercise spiritual leadership. We are in this together, and we are building a community of disciples. We pray at team meetings, and it filters throughout the system. Church people who do not pray and read the Bible together are like Firestone employees who meet and do not mention tires. I am not concerned about providing or controlling the devotional material. I am concerned that as leaders we create a church culture that understands accountability to prayer, Scripture, and caring for one another, as well as getting the job done.

The committee structure was put in place to help us move ahead, and it was really a wonderful gift for the '50s and the '60s. It was a time when committees met to get something done. *Committee* to boomers and busters, however, means a group of people getting together and doing nothing. If we continue to recruit for committees, those older folks who sign up will be looking around wondering why they are still doing all the work. We need to blow up the committee structure and start teaming. You will still need basic boards and committees, but wherever possible form ministry teams instead. Set the teams alongside existing committees. Let momentum from the ministry teams carry your church to many more opportunities by many more lay volunteers.

Creating ministry teams also encourages people to apply imagination to ministry. It used to be when someone wanted to implement a great idea in worship, they came to me. If I liked their idea, I would refer them to Handt Hanson. If Handt thought it was a useful suggestion, he would invite the idea person to a worship committee. Then the committee would meet, and if the committee liked the idea, they would refer it to the church council to get it ratified.

How many people have enough patience to wait three months to get approval for a creative idea? Or how many noes does a person experience in the process? A system is needed that says yes to good ideas.

Effective or Efficient

We also need to choose whether we want to be effective or efficient. I used to believe they were one and the same, but we live in a relational world, and relationships are not efficient. Ministry is highly relational. The issue for us as pastors and leaders is one of *effective relationships,* and since it is not possible to relate effectively to everyone, we need to target the leaders.

It has been my experience that unspoken expectations on the part of either the congregation or the pastoral leaders are usually wrong. We must create the conversation among leadership that clarifies expectations. Then lay leaders need to continue to push and support the changes, helping the pastor to move ahead. It is absolutely critical. Pastors would not be in ministry if they did not care, but we cannot create culture shifts alone. I read recently a sad and disheartening statistic: 7 out of every 10 senior pastors cannot wait to get out. Why? They are still playing Cisco and Pancho. They are still riding in alone.

GIVING AWAY MINISTRY

Our strategy for the future is to give ministry away. God is setting the agenda. We want to win an additional 5,000 people at Prince of Peace. Some of our 9,300 members will never get the new picture. That is OK, but they cannot be allowed to set the agenda. Our job is to be faithful to the Father's agenda. To help people catch His agenda.

Both-And in Place of Either-Or

Try to think of both-and as a foundation for achieving His agenda. If you think only either-or, you are looking through the perspective of the world. Either-or shuts people out. It often makes them harden their categories and choose only one method. Either-or becomes rigid and brittle. It closes minds and dilutes commitments. We are trying to see God's agenda and do His work in more than one way.

In dealing with growth and change, try both-and in place of either-or. It is both traditional and contemporary. If God calls you to empower laity and you are not sure the present membership is willing, do not give up. Rather plant a congregation within your congregation with those people who respond positively. Then guess what will happen? Those involved in the new congregation will drag the others along with them. This means you have positive conflict, which you can ignore as the laity work to solve it.

Kindness to Footdraggers

It is usually inappropriate to tell a member of our church, "You can't be here anymore!" But I can say, "This is what God is calling us to be. This is what we want to do."

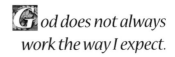

od does not always work the way I expect.

To the footdraggers, I continue with my kindly comments, "You know what? These new members are going to be leading the rest of us one day soon." That approach makes it possible to sidestep some conflict. At the same time, it does not freeze out veteran members. Neither does it divide a church, but it makes it possible for everyone to find their place. The new focus is on the needs of the world around us.

What has been amazing is that some of the most effective ministry started with things I did not like. God does not always work the way I expect. Now when a new ministry proposal is made, I ask only a couple of questions: "Does this square with our mission to welcome, equip, and send? Does it move us toward fulfilling the vision God has called us to achieve?"

One of the most exciting aspects of working with people in the church is discovering their many and various gifts. It is clear to me that God has placed individuals of exceptional gifts around me for a reason. We all win when they are free to do their job. I encourage you to let go of some parts of what you now consider to be your territory and entrust it to others. Trust me—God will give you plenty to do.

When people think they want the pastor present, I think they really want Jesus in their midst, and we know Jesus will come wherever they are. Again, we are changing the mind-set of the church culture. Our task is to see to it that those who go can be the presence of Christ to each other and those they serve. The chaplaincy notion is pastoral care by the dropperful. Instead we can build a community of care to replace a person of care. We need a culture that allows us to consistently care for one another.

As a church grows, the issue of accountability becomes more critical. An Alban Institute study made it clear that one of the reasons people do not want to give time in their church is because they are not accountable. They do not know when they have succeeded. Accountability is telling the truth, not simply acknowledging the effort with thanks. Mutual accountability is not control. It is learning when to let go. It is turning people loose and holding them accountable to the mission and the vision of the church, not to the pastor.

STAFFING FOR LEADERSHIP

In our new system, our No. 1 job is leadership development. We need to stop focusing on doing and begin focusing on being. It is who we are that is our strength. Leaders lead from the inside out. If we can focus on who we are, we will be strong enough to move from being to knowing. By changing the focus from doing to being, we create authenticity within the whole system.

At our church, we used to hire people because they had great skills. Now our focus has changed drastically. We want staff members whose credentials start with devotion to Christ.

The pattern is to move from being to knowing to doing. Look at Jesus, our Savior and Leader. What was the first thing He did every day? He secluded himself to be with God. Then He knew what He was to do, and He went forth and did it.

TRUST IS THE CURRENCY OF MINISTRY

Even as spiritual integrity provides a bedrock foundation for ministry, trust is the currency of ministry. Trust is the new currency for the church. When trust is in place, the people of God respond favorably to every challenge.

Some of the laypeople you trust will become champions for God; others will never catch on to what He is doing. Let your champions establish the norm, and watch your congregation grow healthy. Trust that in the midst of all this noise and rethinking, the Holy Spirit will do the work. Watch what God will do, and hang on for the ride.

∎*3*∎

HOW TO START LAY MOBILIZATION
Initiate This A-C-T-I-O-N Plan

Dale E. Galloway

If you want to see God multiply your congregation's impact, begin to establish a leader-making culture that makes heroes of laypeople who lead ministry groups. Lay mobilization starts and continues by connecting people with ministry and training, and by investing yourself in people you organize into ministry teams.

Only what we share multiplies. When we are serious about advancing the kingdom of God and expanding His Church on earth, we will build teams of laypeople and work through those teams.

PROCESS RATHER THAN ARRIVAL

View lay ministry and lay mobilization as a process of growth rather than as a perfect attainment to be accomplished next month or next year. Those who champion lay ministry should think direction rather than destination. Do not expect lay ministers to be adequate or flawless. They will not be, but they can learn and accomplish incredible achievements for Christ.

Rick Warren's concept that purpose always comes before plan helps me: "Every great church has defined its purpose and then somehow figured out a process or a system for fulfilling those purposes." Note the progression—first a vision of purpose or mission, then church leaders put a process in place that achieves the desired results.

You can start or make more effective the lay mobilization in your church by initiating the following A-C-T-I-O-N plan.

A = Attention

What captures your attention captures you. What captivates the pastor's imagination is what is communicated to congregants. What becomes your passion becomes their priority. Gaining attention of your congregation for lay ministry can be accomplished by these steps.

1. Focus your church members on lay ministry by asking the right questions in the most influential groups. Asking questions is an effective way to use your authority without becoming authoritarian. It's a way to help people develop new understandings without making them feel manipulated.

Typical questions can be: What is authentic ministry for us? What can laypersons do that pastors could never do?

2. Cast vision again and again. Nehemiah is a wonderful biblical example who moved his people from a vision to the implementation of mission. Steinbron in *The Lay-Driven Church* retraces Nehemiah's pattern on this continuum that moves from a dream to its accomplishment:

A. Awareness of need (1:3).
B. Troubled by conditions (1:4).
C. Fasting and talking with God about the need (1:4-5).
D. First action step: articulate the vision to others (2:5).
E. Second action step: gather materials to start (2:11-18).
F. Third action step: cast the vision (2:17-18).
G. Fourth action step: get the people's response (2:18).
H. Fifth action step: begin project by involving others (2:18).
I. Reassurance of the vision from God (2:8, 12, 18, 20).

*incoln revved up
...a battalion of energy
within each person.*

I know a pastor who did this very well in a church that had the old pastor-do-everything paradigm. One of the ways he began to bring subtle changes was by interviewing laypeople in the Sunday worship service. In these interviews, he always inquired about laypersons who had helped the interviewee along their spiritual pilgrimage. Find your own technique. Cast the vision by emphasizing the potential impact laypersons have on other members and friends of your congregation.

In his book *Lincoln on Leadership,* Donald T. Phillips explains the effect of Lincoln's vision on the country: "By clearly renewing his vision and then gaining acceptance and commitment, Lincoln essentially revved up, and then released, what amounted to a battalion of energy within each person. Without question, Lincoln realized what every leader must—that the process of renewal releases the critical human talent and energy that is necessary to insure success" (168). A similar dynamic results from building lay ministry in a congregation.

3. Teach lay ministry from Scripture. The pattern can be found on nearly every page of the New Testament. I especially enjoy teaching Acts 6—8. When you study the Bible with a lay ministry focus, you will discover more material than you can possibly use.

4. Communicate passion for shared ministry. Give laypersons who are involved in ministry high visibility. Use them to help with worship service components. Give them recognition and express appreciation. Develop your paid staff from people who have been effective in lay ministry; that creates a tremendous motivation for others to do effective work.

In all you do, lead with an attitude of gratitude. In Portland, we featured a month every year called the month of gratitude. I would take time in every worship service to introduce some unsung hero the people did not know who served behind the scenes. Try putting your arm around that person, share what they do, have others who do similar ministries stand up, and give them all a big hand.

5. Celebrate lay ministry. As leader, you have the privilege to focus the spotlight of the church on what matters most. What you emphasize is what people believe has high priority. Shine the spotlight on lay ministry, and many will give their energy to it.

C = Connecting People with Ministry

Since lay ministry never happens by accident, it has to be

done with intentional purpose and has to be planned well. Here are ways to help laypersons make these connections:

1. **Teach them how to move from**
   - consumers to servers
   - spectators to participators
   - takers to givers
   - cared for to becoming caregivers
   - unemployed to full employment

Since Christians are born to serve, the morale of any church quickly improves by increasing lay involvement by 20 percent. Service is to the soul what physical exercise is to the body. The tragedy is that too many churches have an alarmingly high rate of unemployment.

2. **Give lay mobilization high priority.** Make it a core value. Tell prospective joiners in every membership class they are expected to serve. Ask them where they want to begin. Do not hesitate or wait. Serving deserves high value both from a biblical as well as the server's perspective.

3. **Put systems in place.** Design a system that connects people with their call, their gifts, and the various opportunities to serve in the Body of Christ.

4. **Help people understand that opportunities to serve often come at unpredictable, even inconvenient, moments.** That is one reason Jesus told the story of the Good Samaritan. His message presses us to consider whether we serve Christ when needed or when it is convenient.

5. **Maximize the congregation's understanding and use of spiritual gifts.** Familiarize yourself with biblical teaching about gifts. Study the rich literature that has been produced on the subject. To make lay ministry work, everyone must be given opportunity to identify their own spiritual gifts and be shown opportunities to use those gifts. Teach and preach on spiritual gifts from Rom. 12:6-8; 1 Cor. 12:4-11, 27-31.

6. **Match ministry and gifts.** After the gifting has been identified, ministry and gifts must be matched. This process applies especially to existing ministry openings in your church. It helps open the door for new ministries you dream of starting. I often envisioned new ministries for several years before we found

the right leader. We waited to start until we found someone who had vision, passion, and needed gifts. Though such a wait may frustrate you, it is considerably less disappointing than starting with a leader who does not have gifts or vision for the task.

The gifting issue also significantly impacts existing ministries that lose their leader. Many pastors and decision groups think that once a program or phase of ministry is started, it must continue forever. That's not true. Some ministries flounder when personnel changes. Some ministries have seasons of effectiveness. Some ministries over time lose their impact and appeal. If you don't have potential leaders who have gifts for a certain ministry, it may be wise to close it down. It is possible there will be a right time to start it again.

Lay Mobilization Requires Serious Recruitment

To implement lay ministry takes serious recruitment commitments from every pastor, staff member, lay leader, and layperson already involved in ministry. Recruitment cannot be reserved for the professionally trained staff. To keep recruitment activities solely in their hands creates a growth bottleneck.

• **Life in order.** Obviously, some system for approving proposed placements must be in place. And those invited to serve must be faithful followers of Jesus with their lives in order.

When people are given total permission to employ their spiritual gifts, they will do better work and they will grow spiritually.

• **Gradual involvement.** Effective recruitment usually begins by getting people to participate at whatever level they are ready to give. Get them started. Let them see what is being done. Help them get close enough to the actual ministry so they begin to think about what they could do and see how much they are needed. Those two components—seeing how it is done and seeing the need firsthand—are two ways God kindles vision for the work.

One of the finest lay pastors at Portland started by taking the offering. That was his first expression of Christian service, but it was a start. Soon he tried something more complicated. He kept growing in commitment as he expanded his vision for ministry. Step by step, he became one of our most effective lay pastors.

• **Permission.** All churches with effective lay ministry grant persons permission to do ministry. Motivation grows when restrictions are kept to a minimum. People respond more quickly to high expectations from their leader than to suspicious gatekeepers. When people are given total permission to employ their spiritual gifts, they will do better work, they will grow spiritually, and they will usually excel beyond anything you could hope for.

To maximize the effectiveness of lay ministry, intentionally develop a spirit inside yourself that responds to a proposal for placing people with "Why not?" rather than "They are not ready."

Permission stimulates action. Restraint hinders ministry. Permission releases and sets free. Restraints make people feel distrusted. Some laypersons with great potential will not even consider doing ministry until they are sure their pastor has given permission for them to move ahead. Creating a climate of permission is one of the most overlooked parts of developing lay ministry.

• **Whole-life ministry.** Teach the whole-life concept of ministry. Trueblood was right when he said, "Secular work well done is a holy enterprise. . . . Work which has no other incentive than a paycheck is closer to slavery than to freedom." The idea is to teach people that their work or profession is their calling for God. That makes their job the primary setting where they carry out their calling. Thus, the call of God to do ministry in the workplace well never changes, even though a layperson's job changes. This is a lived-out expression of Paul's teaching: "Whatever you do, do it all for the glory of God" (1 Cor. 10:31).

What happens when you connect people with their spiritual calling and their gifts for fulfilling that calling either in church or in the world or both? The list is long—people led to Christ, satisfaction, changed lives, ministry multiplied, churches grown, and believers developed.

T = Train

Apply John D. Rockefeller Jr.'s idea of training to ministry: "Good management consists in showing average people how to do the work of superior people" [Louis E. Boone, *Quotable Business,* 19]. At New Hope Community Church, we discovered that rally-type training sessions were needed to reexcite everyone about the vision and keep them moving in the same direction.

Rally-type sessions are not enough. Smaller training meetings are also needed to provide personal attention, for more efficient individual development, and for more effective application of gifts to a specific phase of ministry. Providing these two training levels makes it possible to decentralize ministry and at the same time brings everyone together to keep the central vision in focus. Consider building the following components into your training.

1. Continued general training is essential. When lay ministry starts, the senior pastor can personally give everyone the same basic training. But training must become more specialized as a church grows. In Portland, I saw the day when multiple training sessions were going on during the week, and all staff pastors were doing training with laypersons who worked in their area of specialization.

2. Avoid isolation. A serious difficulty often takes place when a person feels alone or isolated in an assignment. Every lay ministry person needs the excitement of understanding how that ministry contributes to the whole. That's why the rally-type training is so important.

3. Keep the vision central. A central vision needs to be communicated over and over. It grows dim when it is not emphasized. We learned one thing the hard way at New Hope: as we decentralized ministry with 550 lay pastors leading small groups, many of them only dimly saw the vision of the whole church and understood how they fit into it. To correct this weakness, I came to understand that the pastor is the one who must keep recasting the vision so everyone knows how they fit into the big picture.

4. Define what you mean by *lay pastor.* I used the title *pastor* because it is a rich, wonderful, "give it your all" word. I would rather be called Pastor than Reverend, Doctor, or Dean. I believe *pastor* rolls into one word the meaning of shepherd, servant, caregiver, teacher, and minister. The word *lay* in front of the title *pastor* simply means that such people are employed at a secular job to support themselves in addition to their ministry through the church. Lay pastors at New Hope had four functions: (1) evangelist (Matt. 28:18-20); (2) connector (2 Cor. 5:19-20); (3) shepherd (John 21:15-17); and (4) servant (Rom. 12:1).

Lay ministry has a rich heritage in the influences of John Wesley and Frances Asbury. John Wesley trained more than 650 lay preachers during his half century of active ministry. He used lay pastors to conduct the class meetings.

James Garlow, in *Partners in Ministry,* reminds us: "One of Wesley's lay preachers, Francis Asbury, was sent to America in 1771 at 26. He later became the first bishop of American Methodism. The major reason Methodism spread across the county at such an unparalleled pace was Asbury's extensive deployment of lay preachers. Methodism was not the only denomination to grow rapidly in America. The Baptist faith also spread rapidly across the wilderness and prairies. That was likewise due to the extensive use of laity. Alexander Campbell founded a group now known as the Disciples of Christ. Their rapid growth in 19th-century America can also be largely attributed to their emphasis upon the ministry of all of God's people" (77-78).

The bottom line of the connection factor in lay ministry is that you develop a special group of people you especially train to share and multiply ministry.

The greatest frustration in the contemporary church may be the issue of pastoral care. The question is, Can laypersons do pastoral care, and will the people accept it from them? From experience, I know lay pastors can do pastoral care and do it well.

Here's how it worked for us. The New Hope Church model had 550 lay pastors who led small groups. These leaders received initial training, rally training, on-the-job training, and continual training.

The bottom line of the connection factor in lay ministry is that you develop a special group of people you especially train to share and multiply ministry. Then you provide them with a systematic way to carry out ministry and provide pastoral care to everyone connected to their group.

Though I called ours lay pastors, give them any name you wish. The secret is good training and permission to serve in pastoral relationships to a group of about 10 people.

I = Invest Yourself in People

What you give of yourself to developing laypeople for ministry is among the most productive investments you will ever make. It multiples ministry many times over. And the results are impressive and eternal. As you build people, they build the church and stimulate congregational health.

1. Mobilization is more than delegation. Investing in people development is different than delegation. I think of the process as divesting myself of ministry so I have time, energy, and commitment to multiply my ministry through the ministry of others.

2. Investing means mentoring. Think how many different people provided some degree of mentoring in your own emotional, spiritual, and professional development. I think of mentoring as formal and informal investments in other people done in three areas:

- **Disciplines of Christian living.** There are many different ways to help people develop spiritually. This might involve teaching lay leaders how to pray or read the Bible. It may involve helping them discover and experience the biblical teaching of the Spirit-filled life. You might take them with you to an Emmaus Retreat. The method can be determined by the layperson's needs and the mentor's experiences.

- **Development of a person's ministry gifts.** This includes helping individuals discover their gifts and making sure their gifts are matched to a ministry assignment. This kind of mentoring often requires one-on-one conversations about gifts. It is also strengthened by your encouragement to try using their gifts in a particular assignment.

- **Help for laity to become healthy persons.** I did not fully understand this part of mentoring until more recent years. But

I learned the hard way. I had a lay pastor I discipled in ministry. He became a marvelously effective leader who served for 16 years on our staff. God greatly used this person. I helped him develop spiritually. I helped him discover his gifts and match them to ministry opportunities. I showed him how to do ministry, and he did it so well. Sadly, I did not give enough attention to his emotional well-being. Some of his negative childhood experiences finally overwhelmed him. By the time I realized what was happening, he was so depressed that it took him out of the ministry. I missed his need and my opportunity to help.

Potential lay leaders must be taught how to live a balanced life so they can be at their best in ministry.

More and more, in a society that has so much brokenness, we must help the people we train to become whole. If issues and pain from their own past are not settled, they become broken people ministering to broken people. That means we soon have churches filled with broken, dysfunctional people. Potential lay leaders must be taught how to live a balanced life so they can be at their best in ministry.

O = On Ministry Teams

A team always accomplishes more than one person can do alone. Isolation in lay ministry is among the biggest causes of dropout. That is why the senior pastor must teach small-group leaders to minister to each other before they minister to others. For lasting effectiveness, a ministry team needs encouragement, accountability, and affirmation from others within their group.

Build this idea into all you do with lay ministry—no one should be alone in ministry. As Scripture teaches, the church functions best when it works together as a Body of Christ—every part performs its own functions. In relationships in the small group, everyone gives care and everyone receives care. The resulting spiritual synergism will amaze you.

Everyone needs the power of a team to encourage them. For example, I am always strengthened when our distinguished clergy council meets at the Beeson Center. The main purpose of this group is to serve as advisers for our various programs. However, as we gather around the conference table, our chairman starts the meeting by saying, "Let's minister to each other." Then we spend about 45 minutes going around the table, sharing our lives, and praying for one another. Your lay ministry leaders need similar experiences so they will not burn out.

N = Now

Complacency is the biggest hindrance to starting lay ministry. Many of us like things the way they are. Some of us might be willing to change a little if it did not require too much effort. Complacency, however, doesn't fit with dynamic words used throughout this chapter like *revolution* and *reformation*. To transform your church into an effective lay ministry center, complacency must be challenged by emphasizing the Bible's urgency. These passages are passionate and impressive:

"Behold, now is the day of salvation" (2 Cor. 6:2, RSV).

"I must work the works of him that sent me, while it is day" (John 9:4, KJV).

"Behold, I have set before you an open door" (Rev. 3:8, RSV).

"Open your eyes and look at the fields! They are ripe for harvest" (John 4:35).

"So send I you" (John 20:21, KJV).

"Therefore go and make disciples of all nations" (Matt. 28:19).

The time has come to make it happen. Do it now.

GO FOR THE BENEFITS

Lay ministry means multiplying effectiveness. Lay ministry means teaching others to do ministry. Lay ministry means strengthening all the people you serve. Lay ministry means training folks. Lay ministry especially means helping others take the baton from your hand to multiply ministry now and to continue ministry long after you are gone.

Lori, one of my doctor of ministry students, is a national conference speaker. Her focus is high school students. Through her organization she focuses on building character in the public schools. She tells about a time when she was cutting up on the back row in a college class. The professor, a lady who had never married, said, "I want to see you after class."

So Lori went up after the class, and the teacher said, "Tomorrow I want you to sit on the front row. I want you to come on time. I want you to listen to everything I say."

Lori responded, "Well, I'll drop the class, since this is an elective."

But the teacher said, "You won't drop because you need what I have to give you. God is going to greatly use your life to help thousands of people, and you need what I share in this class."

So Lori moved to the front row. She took other classes from this teacher. The instructor became her strong mentor across many years. Wherever Lori went into ministry, she often called her former teacher and asked for prayers.

One day, Lori learned her faithful mentor was hospitalized. She immediately canceled her schedule and went to visit. After they exchanged greetings, her mentor, who lay dying, said, "I never had a child. But if I had a daughter, I would want her to be just like you. God has greater things yet for your life. Here, I want you to take my hand and take the baton."

Telling the story, Lori confessed, "I didn't want that responsibility. But she kept saying, 'Take the baton.'"

Lori took her hand and the invisible baton, and the teacher died.

Since that day, she's gone on to mentor thousands of youth through her ministry. Lori has been aware that she has to carry on the task she has been given. In many ways, she helps carry on the work of her teacher and friend.

That is lay ministry's bottom line. It is a powerful way to pass the baton to those who will multiply ministry where we are and where we will never go, and then continue ministry after our demise.

▪4▪

NICHE-PICKIN'–NEW PARADIGM FOR LAY MINISTRY
The Frazer Church Volunteer Model

John Ed Mathison

An insightful observer suggested that the greatest thing that could happen to any church was for the Holy Spirit to move in, for preachers to move over, and for layfolk to move out into the world to serve. Traditionally, one of the biggest problems regarding lay mobilization is us—the pastors. We want to keep our hands on everything. We are afraid of losing control. We want to be in charge and look over everything. Many of the worst offenders do not even realize what a tight lid they keep on service opportunities. With all my heart I believe the most important characteristic of being an authentic church is how willingly we share significant ministry with lay believers.

How can we pastors liberate laity to do ministry?

Most of us think we have all the answers and possess all the creative ideas. We don't. Many times the best ideas for service come from a janitor or other common people. Layfolk are loaded with creative ideas of ministry, but they do not always feel free to share them.

HAVE YOU HEARD ABOUT NICHE-PICKIN'?

The important vehicle used at Frazer Church to involve laity in service to Christ is called "niche-pickin'." We believe everybody has a niche God has given them, and each person is encouraged to pick their niche. We place full responsibility on individual members to pick their niche of service.

51

You will have less nit-picking when you have good niche-pickin'. It works like this. When laypeople pick a niche that uses their spiritual gifts and find a ministry that matters to them, they lose interest in nit-picking. An important principle for Christian service is contained in the old saying "You can't row and rock the boat at the same time." The more layfolk involve themselves in meaningful ministry, the more they discover how exciting it is to serve Christ. The more people give themselves to service, the less backbiting you will experience. Niche-pickin' means people volunteer for service rather than being recruited to do something they are not sure they want to do.

The basic but transforming idea for the church and individual members—believers volunteer for service rather than being recruited.

WHY DO LAY MINISTRY IN YOUR CHURCH?

This basic question is essential to all a church is and does. It is no secret that many contemporary churches expect paid staff to do all the ministry—but no matter how large, a staff can never do every phase of ministry that needs to be done. There is never enough money to hire staff to do everything. That is one reason why lay ministry is experiencing such an impressive renewal these days.

• **Lay ministry is biblical.** The Protestant Reformation closed the impassable gulf between what clergy and laity can do in the church. We have almost re-created the gulf again. From beginning to end, Scripture makes no difference between clergy and laity. The privilege and responsibility belong to all.

At Frazer Church, the biblical model from 1 Cor. 12 is used for lay ministry. Paul uses the illustration of the human body for the Church, citing that the Body of Christ has many different parts. Each part has a specific function, a job to perform that the whole Body really needs. All the parts working together make my body serve me effectively. Likewise, the Body of Christ on earth functions best when every part performs its functions effectively. An alarming part of our problem, however, is that many parts of church bodies are dysfunctional. The feet won't go where they are needed, the hands won't do their work, and the Body falls flat on its face.

Isn't that a picture of many congregations you know about? Folks going in all different directions at the same time. In the process, those congregations become lame or spastic. Then they fall or become crippled. Biblically, every member has been given a gift, and God wants it used.

In the niche-pickin' system, every believer is urged to find the place where they fit and get to work.

• **Lay ministry is practical.** Consider the 80/20 principle—that means 20 percent of the folks do 80 percent of the work in the average church. Now, it doesn't take a rocket scientist to figure what a church could accomplish if the idle 80 percent went to work. Think of the spiritual impact such service would have on those who serve—their spiritual lives would be revolutionized.

In most churches, the pastor and/or staff go to people they know who are going to do something or who are already doing something. They give them more to do. As a result, many ministries of service are done poorly by overworked people. The bottom line is ineffectiveness for the church and missed blessing for the inactive.

Niche-pickin', however, allows the other 60, 70, or 80 percent to figure out what their gifts are. It helps them identify where they can most effectively use their gifts. Even more important, it helps them know where God wants their gifts used and helps them discover how they can do it best.

Let me share a disturbing statistic. If people who join a church do not become involved in the first six months in a meaningful ministry and a small group, 50 percent of them will become permanently inactive.

That's vastly different from the way it once was. Thirty years ago, folks joined a church, and they attended every Sunday because worship was significant to them and there were not as many other things to do outside the church. In fact, the church did not have much competition for their attendance and their finances. That has changed in today's culture, so people must be involved quickly. The goal is to have 100 percent of church members doing some form of ministry.

• **Lay ministry is productive.** Think of the multiplication lay ministry gives a church. A pastor can visit 4 homes in one evening. When that same pastor trains 40 folks to make 4 visits, 160 homes get visited!

Let me share several examples of increased productivity at Frazer Church.

Nearly everyone who comes to our church enjoys the food we serve. All of this is possible because some of our people niche-pick to do food service. Some work in food service who can't teach, sing, or do prison ministry. Our whole food ministry means somebody prayed, "Lord, where do You want me?" Then they felt led to the food serving niche.

This church served 2,700 meals a week last year. We don't have a dietician. We don't have a cooking staff for the kitchen. Basically, this work is done by about 400 persons who volunteer each year to help with food service.

Most Christian leaders are quick with math. Check the numbers. If we had to hire food personnel, we would need 8 to 10 folks, and that cost would be a big budget item. When members volunteer, however, two important things are accomplished. You give people opportunity to utilize their talent. You also free up money to be used in other ministries.

Lay ministry done right also has many staff implications. One important implication—the more a church has laypersons volunteering for meaningful ministry, the less staff it needs.

Here is another example of achievement that goes beyond savings in the budget. About four years ago, three laymen came to my office to say, "Pastor, have you heard about Promise Keepers? We'd like to take a group to Indianapolis."

My first question was, "What's Promise Keepers?"

"Well, it's this organization for men."

I pointed out that Indianapolis is 11 hours away.

They said, "Well, we'd like to take a group of men there."

I half jokingly said, "Fine. Hope you can get some to go." I figured they might get a carload.

They said, "Well, we've already reserved 12 buses."

"Who in the world is going on 12 buses?" I asked.

"Well, the men are going to get excited about it."

Staffwise, we spent almost no time on Promise Keepers. Laity who had the vision found the niche. They did well. The first two on the bus were my son and me. They also needed 14 buses to care for the crowd—2 more than they planned.

The next year they went to Atlanta. The local television station came to take pictures of all the buses. It became the talk of the town. I think 30 buses were needed that year.

ay ministry can be amazingly productive.

Laypeople did it. What a blessing they have been to this church. Many marriages have been saved and others strengthened. In our church, wives sign up their husbands. They say it is the best thing that ever happened to their families.

The strong point I want to make is that lay ministry can be amazingly productive. No church needs as many staff persons when you release a whole cadre of talented, gifted, creative layfolk who figure out what needs to be done and do it.

• **Lay ministry identifies leaders.** As we developed lay ministry at Frazer, I discovered many more potential leaders with much more capability than I expected. In most congregations, there are more potential leaders than we realize. Laypeople have more talent, ability, creativity, and commitment than many pastors think. Often they do not come forward because they think we want to control everything and that we want to be the initiator of every new idea in the church. Often they are right in those assessments.

In all honesty, laypeople at Frazer often have a much bigger vision for the church than I do. Some of them have a God-inspired vision that shames me. Sometimes I have to just get on board and follow their vision. We have to release control, trust them, and allow them to fulfill God's dream for His Church.

OUR SECRET: VOLUNTEERS, NOT RECRUITS

Consider this word—*volunteers*. Walk around it. Consider it seriously and spiritually. Do you have the word clearly in your mind—*volunteers*?

Most churches recruit people to do various tasks. At Frazer, we do not recruit anybody to do anything. Rather we say to every member, "As a follower of Jesus, you are expected to volunteer to serve someplace in the life of the church." Then they are given the opportunity to freely decide where they will serve.

Beyond Guilt and Intimidation

Most preachers know how to use guilt and intimidation. Guilt tells the prospective worker how much he or she is needed. Church leaders may remind such a one that someone did it for him or her. We pastors sometimes suggest that someone has to take this class or your children may not have a teacher.

Intimidation is sometimes the weapon of choice. A pastor puts the fear of the Lord into people: "You know, God told me you should do this, and if you don't do it, He might be very displeased with you."

Alternative to Recruitment

In place of recruitment, I propose our church's concept of volunteering be considered.

Note first one of the difficult dimensions of recruitment the way it is often done. If pastors and staff members have to recruit persons, that means those leaders have to be smart enough to know what everyone should do. Smart staff folks like that are hard to find. When laypersons are asked to prayerfully consider their gifts, however, and allow God to lead them to employ those gifts, it is amazing how God places people in specific areas of need in the church.

Let me share a story about how God uses niche-pickers. Several years ago, a lady from our church approached a football player from Auburn. She kept trying to get him to attend Sunday School. He replied politely but firmly, "I don't go to Sunday School." She and her husband stayed after him, and the guy told them again, "No, I don't do Sunday School." Finally, to quiet her invitations, he challenged her, "If you'll teach a Sunday School class, I'll go." This woman is about the least likely person to teach an adult Sunday School class you have ever met—certainly not the kind of person a pastor would ask to start a class that might attract football stars. She's an elementary school music teacher. Though she was an unlikely prospect for such an assignment, it is amazing what God does. To get the football player to attend, she started the class.

Frazer Church has a policy that the biggest classes get the biggest rooms. Since it started, her Sunday School class has been through most rooms in the church. They have grown so large, they have to meet in the sanctuary—the only space large enough to seat them. Two hundred plus attend.

Niche-pickin' takes the place of recruitment. This unlikely person, whom I would never have considered to start an adult Sunday School class, assessed what she could do and picked her niche.

A man with a black belt in karate joined the church last year on profession of faith. He said to me, "Pastor, I understand I'm supposed to volunteer for something. I'm a black belt in karate. I've been praying for God's direction. What I would like to do is teach a class on self-defense for women and charge a fee. If you charge them, they will think it is more important and they will come. Then you can give the money to the college ministry for their mission work. What do you think?"

Though I had strong misgivings, I said, "Sounds like a great idea."

He said, "Good. I've already scheduled the first class."

He began teaching women self-defense. He had just become a Christian and joined the church. He had been baptized and was excited about serving others.

A young, divorced woman took that class and learned a lot about self-defense. Two weeks later, she was jogging at a nearby park when she heard another woman screaming for help. She looked around and concluded nobody was around to help but her. Then she realized this screaming woman was being attacked by a man trying to rape her.

The jogger thought about what she had learned in class. Fearlessly, she started running toward the rapist with such authority that he ran for his life. Later he was arrested, and evidence showed he had raped 11 women in our community, 2 from our church.

This all happened because somebody volunteered to do something many pastors might not think fits into the church framework. As a result, this young woman took what she learned and employed it to save another woman.

This story demonstrates that you never know what God will use when you allow opportunities for people to volunteer as the Lord leads them.

FIVE-DIMENSION COMMITMENT CARD

This is how we recruit lay ministers. In the fall of the year, we distribute a five-phase card that calls for commitment to prayer, attendance, witness, service, and giving.

In the service section of the card, we list about 200 different ministries, a kind of ministry menu. The card always lists specific ministry needs and opportunities, but at the bottom it says "other." If a person believes God has gifted him or her to do something that is not on that list, he or she is asked to write it in. If the proposed ministry does not fit into our three-word mission statement—win, disciple, serve—the church does not fund or sponsor the activity. This "other" category helps stimulate the creative process for new ministries. It gives everyone permission to think of new, innovative ways to do ministry. Some of our most effective ministries started as an "other" that was not on the commitment card ministry list. Ideally, the commitment card helps everyone in the church in three ways: (1) it serves as a checklist of what is needed; (2) it serves as a permission for church members to think in new categories; and (3) it helps the church staff think in new paradigms about how ministry can be done.

This card is a commitment card, not an interest survey. People know that when they check an area of service on the card, they for one year commit to that ministry.

All of these concerns are combined with financial commitment on one card. How many times have you heard church members say, "The only time the church comes to see me is when they want money"? That can't be said in our congregation. Each fall, an every-member canvass takes us to visit everybody in their homes, but we go as much for a commitment of time and where they want to serve as we go for money. We ask people to commit to their church during the year. We ask them, "Would you write down how many folks you are going to point to Christ during the year?" That's more important than money. The church counts on their commitment, and they know it. In volunteering on that card, they are then giving much more than a lukewarm interest. It's a genuine though voluntary commitment.

Our volunteer system solves some problems before they arise. Take Vacation Bible School as an example. It's a wonderful, concentrated effort to get Christian teaching into a child's mind, and I doubt if anyone questions its value. The problem for most of us, however, is to get VBS volunteers when we most need them. Note the beauty of the commitment card for solving this personnel problem. In October or November the card says, "Teach Vacation Bible School." At that time, God leads enough folks to teach Bible school for the coming June. When the time comes in spring to begin planning for VBS, the teachers have already committed. Since God has led people to volunteer in November, all we have to do is train them in the spring, and they are prepared to do their ministry through Vacation Bible School.

Annual Commitment Renewal

Everyone understands at our church that every commitment is for a year. Everyone revolunteers each year. Everyone knows they can change or recommit every year. The process makes it possible to switch to a new area of service or to reaffirm the one where they now serve.

One of the biggest problems with recruitment in many churches is that folks know that if they say yes, they are likely to be stuck with the same assignment until they resign or die. To avoid a "forever feeling" commitment, everyone at Frazer is asked to volunteer for only a year. Everyone knows if one aspect of service does not work, they can volunteer for something else later.

Cuts Down on Burnout

Ministry literature for laity and clergy is filled with discussions about burnout. The newspaper in our city did an interesting story on potential burnout among volunteers in the church. They interviewed me and said, "You have a lot of them at Frazer. Tell me about their burnout experiences." I had never thought about it before. As the reporter visited with me, I suddenly realized I didn't know of any volunteer in our church who felt burned out. I thought I might not be listening carefully enough, though, so I suggested to the reporter, "You need to talk to other staff people." He did. None of us could come up with a single layperson who said, "I'm burned out."

Why was that? I think I know. It's hard to burn out if God gives you a gift and leads you to pick the place where you use that gift to do ministry and where you feel fulfilled doing it.

The volunteer concept gives folks an opportunity to invest their lives in something that makes a difference in the church and the world. That leads to satisfaction in service rather than burnout.

What If No One Volunteers?

This volunteering idea, of course, takes some risks. If nobody volunteers, we assume God doesn't want His church to do that ministry, so we don't do it. As hard as it is, a ministry gets shut down if no one volunteers.

In most churches, too much time, energy, and money are spent doing things that are no longer needed or attended. Such ministries sometimes need a memorial service and a decent burial.

Choosing Leaders

In spite of the niche-pickin' emphasis in our church, no one volunteers to be a leader or chairperson of anything. These leaders are selected. No one can come in and say, "I'm volunteering to be chairman of the Finance Committee next year," or "I volunteer to be chairman of the Council on Ministries." Volunteering has to do with serving. Volunteering is deciding where God is leading you as a believer to serve.

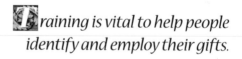

raining is vital to help people identify and employ their gifts.

Leaders are chosen. One of the most important things I do as a senior pastor is to select leaders. The Nominating Committee nominates leaders, and the pastor chairs the Nominating Committee in the Methodist Church. That means the pastor has lots of input into who the leaders will be. Sadly, many people in the church are more interested in who is to be the leader than in what is done. That issue leads to many problems with misuse of organizational power and often cripples a church's achievement.

Under the niche-pickin' system, the process of volunteering for service and selecting for leadership makes the Nominating Committee's work easy and efficient because no one is nominated for chairman of a ministry where they have never served. Consequently, leaders are almost always volunteers before they are selected to be leaders. That insures stronger lay leaders throughout the church.

Another part of leadership development is our policy that no one can chair anything for more than two years. That means that after a few years, each ministry has seasoned volunteers who were once leaders of this ministry. This policy also means that the current chairperson knows if he or she is going to enjoy achievement in the area of ministry being led, the leader will need to get started early after being selected. The two-year rule provides a church with three significant strengths: (1) leaders never have enough time to develop seniority ownership notions that stifle some churches; (2) leaders tend to work harder quicker; and (3) leadership assignments tend to be viewed more as service opportunities rather than control strangulations.

It is important to realize, however, that training is vital to help people identify and employ their gifts.

How Is It Actually Done?

A system of volunteering for service gives people many opportunities to discover their gifts and provides a way to use their gifts in satisfying service. The amazing adventure of the system is that as leader you never, never know how God will use folks who are allowed to volunteer and plug into a specific place of service.

Often I am asked how we started this way of thinking and behaving at Frazer. I explain it like this. When I became pastor at Frazer, I was the only staff person. So when I started our ministry together with the lay leaders, none of us knew much about niche-pickin'. We grew into it prayerfully, and it has emerged over the years. Of course, we had some resistance—every church has resistance to aspects of change and stretching. We worked, however, at making it work. The process has been tailored and redesigned many times to meet new demands.

All the while, however, one constant concept has been our cornerstone—God uses lay volunteers more effectively if they are given opportunity to match service responsibilities with their spiritual giftedness. This way of thinking started in my mind when laypersons began to suggest more involvement, and it evolved. The idea is not hard to sell lay leaders because they feel the same frustrations that clergy feel in the way service assignments are filled and controlled in most churches.

God Gives Assignments

In this way of doing things, God actually does the assigning. People do not necessarily pick the niche all by themselves. God calls and assigns volunteers. In His calling He sometimes leads somebody to do some of the tougher jobs.

Outside ushering is a good example of hard work. That is a tough job here in Alabama where summer temperature climbs to 105 degrees, and winter temperature sometimes goes down to 15. That means when worshipers drive into the parking lot, they are not always pleasant when an outside usher approaches their car in the heat or cold and tells them to park in the next row. In spite of hardships, however, a wonderful crew of men and women get to the church as early as 6:30 on Sunday morning to direct traffic. Since God assigned them this specific place, they are faithful, helpful, and cheerful.

A funny incident happened at our back entrance where a new outside usher was posted. He had been instructed to route everybody who drove through his area to the back parking lot. Those who instructed him actually meant folks coming off the Atlanta highway, but he did not realize that. When a lady drove out of the neighboring apartment complex, he routed her through our parking lot. She was on her way to another church for the first time. When she was directed into our parking lot, she tried to get his attention. He thought she was waving, so he waved back and said, "Come on, lady, right through here."

To minimize confusion, she decided she would drive through the parking lot and back onto the street, but there was another usher directing her into the lot. Again she stopped to explain, but the second outside usher misunderstood and waved her into a parking space. Somebody then opened her door and welcomed her to our church. She decided it would be easier to go into the building and then come back out and leave. As she walked up to the door, a friend from her place of work welcomed her. Her friend took charge and said, "Hey, I'm glad you're here. Come on and go to my Sunday School class with me." Her coworker took her by the arm, and before she knew it, she was in a friendly Sunday School class. Since then, that woman has been at our church every Sunday. She even joined our congregation recently.

Laypeople Possess Amazing Creativity

I had no idea of the innate creativity layfolk possess for ministry. In every congregation many extremely creative individuals are waiting for a place to use their talents.

Let me share several amazing examples.

A lady dog trainer came to a staff member and said, "Did you know elderly people sometimes relate to animals better than to people?" The staff pastor replied with a smile, "I didn't know that."

The dog trainer continued, "I've been thinking God might help us use animals to minister to the elderly."

The dog trainer then asked, "Could you put a small announcement in the bulletin to see if anyone else is interested?"

I said, "Fine. You can meet over here in this small room with all the folks who respond." I thought she might have 3 or 4, but 60 responded. They decided to call their ministry PAWS—Pets Are Working Saints. They take a little rabbit, a billy goat, a dog, and a cat to see persons in care facilities. They dress animals up like dolls and go out to nursing homes. We received a thick stack of letters from doctors who told us, "Your PAWS ministry opened up verbal communication with autistic patients that we have never been able to get to speak."

This ministry began because of one creative lay lady who made us laugh at her idea when she took volunteering seriously.

Her group also uses animals in our prison ministry. Some animals have even visited death row. Two men on death row had never spoken to anyone since their incarceration. They began talking to animals our church people brought. Following that breakthrough, the chaplain was able to help a prisoner accept Christ before he was executed. All this was possible because of a layperson with a small animal in a church where creative volunteerism is cherished and encouraged. When laypeople are allowed to decide what they can do, it is unbelievable how much creativity they bring to the work of God, and it is amazing the things they can do.

Here is another incident. A concerned father said, "Pastor, have you ever thought about the problem kids have when they go from sixth to seventh grade? It's a big transition from elementary school to junior high school. It's tough becoming a teenager. I don't know any church doing anything about that transition."

I replied, "I don't either. In fact, I don't know any church that even tries."

He asked, "Could we pray about this issue? Would it be all right if some of us put some ideas together as a possible ministry to this age-group?"

I agreed and said, "Go to work on it."

They prayed and worked. They came up with a helpful ministry called Metamorphoses—for the sixth to seventh grade transition. I cannot adequately describe what that ministry has accomplished. Sixth-grade kids have shown up in droves and are bringing unchurched friends. They love what is happening, and so do I.

Recently I had a parent say, "Pastor, we have a problem with our son. He's been interested in soccer since he was five, and he's on a premier soccer team—the kind of team that travels even in the sixth grade. Our son said, 'Hope you are not disappointed, but I've got to give up soccer.'"

The parents asked, "Why?"

He said, "Well, the coach said we had to practice on Wednesday night, and that's the night of my Metamorphoses group. My church is more important to me than soccer. I'm going to have to give up the team."

I don't hear that much at our church. We also had five boys tell their parents, "We are going to have to give up basketball. It involves Wednesday nights, and that's our church night. We love basketball, but we'd rather be at church."

Last Christmas, my wife and I attended a party on a Tuesday night for a company owned by a man in our church. A couple I didn't know came up to us and said, "You have created a problem in our home." He said, "Our son has buddies who have been taking him to something at your church called Meterah . . ."

I said, "Metamorphoses."

They said, "That's it, that's it. Today is our son's birthday, and we couldn't have his party tonight because we had this business meeting. So we suggested a big party to celebrate his becoming a teenager on Wednesday night."

They continued, "Our son said, 'No, I don't want a party on Wednesday night!'"

We asked, "Why not?"

He said, "That's my church night."

Those parents have never been to church.

They continued, "We said, 'You mean you're giving up a birthday party to go to church?'"

He said, "Yes sir, that's a lot more important. I can have a birthday party the rest of my life."

One of the little girls in the Metamorphoses group has been taking tennis lessons and loves it. She has been saving for months to buy a tennis racket. In her Metamorphoses, she decided to give all the money she had been saving to her group's mission project.

These changes in sixth graders have happened because some layfolk had a dream of something God wanted them to do. They took the time and effort to niche-pick a new ministry. They are making an eternal difference in many lives—children as well as parents.

Every church has committed people who would do similar things if given permission to think new thoughts for God.

Training Is Needed

At our church, the whole month of January is devoted to training. Our church year begins February 1, and the every-member commitment campaign is held during November. Everyone who volunteers in November is asked to take training during January. We use the selected leaders or chairpersons, with the help of the staff, to do the training. Training does several important things: (1) it affirms that what you do is important; (2) it communicates that you—the volunteer—are important; (3) it shows that the church wants you to do your service to Christ well. It also confirms the niche God led the volunteer to pick.

Ownership Encourages Tenacity

When laypeople are allowed to have ownership of a ministry, they give time, energy, and money to make it happen.

When a pastor owns an idea, you know what laity often do? They think and sometimes say, "That's a great idea, Pastor. You do it."

When they own the idea, however, they will see that the work gets done. You know who gets the satisfaction? They do. You know who gets the joy? They do. Joy and satisfaction in service builds character and Christlikeness in them; it also makes them niche-pick other service in the future.

Two Niche-Pickers' Testimonies

Dr. Tom Goodman, my physician who keeps me healthy, came to me and said, "Our church has a big ministry going down on Bell Street in the inner city. There are many people in that part of town who do not get much medical care."

He continued, "I wonder if could we start a medical clinic? I'd like to donate some time to develop a medical clinic ministry down on Bell Street." I encouraged him to pray about the issue, listen to God, and look for others the Lord might be calling to this specialized ministry.

He started praying with a few others. Soon they found pharmaceutical representatives who could get medicines donated. They set up their clinic in an abandoned Methodist church that has sort of been taken over for our ministry. Every Wednesday afternoon, he and his wife, Debbie, and several other layfolk go down to help give medical care to sick people. They pass out tracts and make it an unapologetically Christian clinic that deals with physical as well as spiritual healing.

Here is how Dr. Goodman describes his experience on Bell Street at the clinic he founded: "I've been a family physician for many years. But when we joined Rudy Heinzelman's Sunday School class and began to pray, we started to grow in remarkably new ways in our faith. We signed up to serve. On our annual commitment card, we indicated that we were interested in starting a clinic at our church's ministry center on Bell Street. I thought God was calling us to bless others. But He blessed me well beyond anything I have done for others. And I am grateful."

His wife, Debbie, started an SOS group for children. Here's how she describes her experience: "SOS stands for Sunshine Outlasts Storms. It is a recovery group for children who have suffered a loss of a parent through death or divorce. I signed up and started to work. But I cannot express how much God has blessed me in this effort. For the first time, I have been able to look at a divorce in my past as a broken experience God could use instead of it being a constant reminder of many bad choices I made earlier in my life. God helped me use my hurts to bless children who were struggling with their parents' separation and divorce. I've had boys and girls say they used to think they were the reason their mommy and daddy got divorced. But they don't think that anymore because at SOS they were taught that it's not so.

"God has turned my pain into victory, so I can tell children that even though their mother and father may disappoint them, their Father in heaven loves them. I tell them there is nothing in this life that God cannot make into a blessing if they turn it over to Him."

Debbie continued, "I encourage every pastor to see the potential of the painful things people have in their pasts that God can transform into blessings for others through them."

That's one of the wonderful examples for effective Christian service the niche-pickin' plan makes possible at Frazer Church.

Niche-pickin' is committed to helping people find joy in service—the best pay anyone can receive on earth. At the same time, it assures people they will hear God say, "Well done. Good job!"

CAUTION AND CHALLENGE

I suggest a caution and a challenge. They take us back to the start of this chapter. I fear that we pastors have become one of the largest stumbling blocks to our church's progress. It is our subtle desire to be in control—apparently some prefer to control 50 laypeople than to serve 500 liberated laypeople. If you insist on control, you will never have a liberated laity that uses its creativity and commitment to go all out to do great works for God.

If you question whether you are a controller or not, wrestle with this statement: If I know everything that is going on in my church, there isn't enough going on.

Here's the key to greater effectiveness and growth. If you trust laypeople and they trust you, you can set them free to do unbelievable accomplishments for God. The caution is the control needs of the pastor. The challenge is to set laity free to think, create, and do great things for the King.

■5■

PURPOSE-DRIVEN LAY TRAINING
Equipping Christian Revolutionists

Jim Garlow

A number of years ago during graduate work, I became fascinated with the Wesleyan movement. John Wesley probably had the most extensive network of laypersons trained for ministry ever known in Christian history. Yet Wesley received enormous criticism, especially for his deployment of laypersons to do ministry. During his lifetime, far more was written *against* him than *for* him. His idea of using the laity was too radical for that time. His movement bordered on being a revolution in terms of his use of laity for actually doing ministry.

I was fascinated to read that he trained 653 lay preachers during his ministry; 57 percent stayed with him until his death or their death. The attrition rate of converts substantially dropped with the number of laypeople he trained over the years. These numbers do not even count the thousands of laypersons he called local preachers, trustees, and band leaders, who were such a significant part of his ministry.

Wesley did not intentionally develop this idea of using laity. In fact, he came to accept it while fighting and screaming. It happened after one of his travels, as he returned late to London. Thomas Maxfield, a layperson, had preached in his absence and then dismissed the people. Wesley was furious.

On his way to rebuke Thomas Maxfield, he stopped to see his mother, Susanna. She, his theological mentor as well as his mother, told him, "Rebuke Maxfield if you would, but he is every bit as called of God as you are."

He never did rebuke Thomas Maxfield. Instead, he began to train an army of laypersons for effective Christian service. Their influence and impact can be seen around the world to this day.

The Primary Biblical Foundation

If laypersons are to enjoy a fruitful ministry, training is an absolute necessity. A properly balanced view of lay ministry stresses the lay call to ministry and the lay gifts for ministry as well as training for how to do ministry. Lay training should be intentionally designed and taught with clear objectives, goals, and methods. Those who provide training must always keep in mind that training is offered to enable laypersons to fulfill their call and to multiply many times over what professional clergy are able to do.

Missionary E. Stanley Jones clarified the new purpose for lay training: "The laity, on the whole, have been in the stands as spectators, and the clergy have been on the field playing the game. . . . the laity must come out of the stands as spectators and take the field as players; and the clergymen must come off the field as players and take the sidelines as coaches of a team" (Whitney J. Dough, comp. and ed., *Sayings of E. Stanley Jones*, 96).

This view of training can be traced to Eph. 4. Verse 11 says (NASB): "And He gave some as apostles, and some as prophets, and some as evangelists, and some as pastors and teachers." Then in verse 12 Paul outlines the purpose of the roles mentioned in verse 11: "for the equipping of the saints for the work of service, to the building up of the body of Christ."

The word "equipping" (mobilizing or outfitting) that occurs in Eph. 4 first appears in the New Testament when Jesus was walking along the shores of Galilee. He sees two sets of brothers, Peter and Andrew, James and John, who were mending their nets. That is the same word used here—mending or perfecting—making their nets serve the function for which they were created.

That Eph. 4 passage is a radical call to a lay ministry revolution. Out of my study of Wesley I began to ask, "What were the dynamics of this Wesley revival in terms of laity ministry?" It's transoceanic. It crosses the Atlantic and moves across 250 years to our time. Out of that study grew these four basic principles.

PRINCIPLE 1—LAITY, IF THEY ARE BIBLICALLY PERCEIVED, ARE CALLED INTO THE MINISTRY

The university where I did my undergraduate work had a religion building, and next to it was a psychology building. Separate buildings for business, music, and physical education were also there. But the people who walked into our building were referred to as those who had been called to the ministry. The assumption was that everybody who went to the other buildings was "not called."

It was the thesis of John Wesley that God could do extraordinary things with ordinary believers.

Clearly this is not a scriptural understanding of the nature of a call to ministry. If you are in Christ Jesus, you are called into ministry. Not all are called to preach or give leadership in a church, but every Christian is called into the ministry. Francis Ayers, an Episcopalian, states in *The Ministry of the Laity,* "If you are in Christ, you are called into ministry regardless of how that statement strikes you. You may be pleased, acquiescent, scornful or even irate. It makes no difference. If you are in Christ Jesus, you have been called into the ministry" (25).

Ordinary People Are Used by God

It was the thesis of John Wesley that God could do extraordinary things with ordinary believers. That was the genius of the Wesley revolution. Or as Paul Claudill says in his book, "God writes straight with crooked lines." It's the capacity of God to take otherwise broken lives and do something through them that is inexplicable, because everyone is called into the ministry.

In 1 Pet. 2:4-5, the apostle writes, "And coming to Him as to a living stone which has been rejected by men, but is choice and precious in the sight of God, you also, as living stones, are being built up as a spiritual house for a holy priesthood, to offer up spiritual sacrifices acceptable to God through Jesus Christ" (NASB).

These verses give amazing titles to the church: "living stones" and "a spiritual house for a holy priesthood." Verses 9 and 10 add more titles: "a chosen race," "a royal priesthood," "a holy nation," "a people for God's own possession."

What would happen if believers in every church came to understand these titles are for them? Most of our people, when they think of priest, think of an Anglican or Episcopalian or Catholic clergyman. According to the Bible, a *royal* priesthood means serving the King of Kings.

Laypeople Become Priests of God

Laypeople in our churches need to understand the precise definition of a priest. A priest is a go-between connecting God and the world. A priest in this scriptural passage is one passionately in love with the Lord, who stands between Him and a world that desperately needs to know Him. So the go-between priest looks at the world and says, "My goodness," almost with disgust or anger, "I cannot believe how they are so bent on self-destruction. I cannot believe how bad it is." And then he turns to God in desperation and frustration and says, "You ought to see this mess down here. It's awful. It's terrible." God beckons him to come closer to listen instead of speaking, and He whispers in his ear. The priest starts to nod, a slight smile coming to his face; he turns back around and says, "Ah, world, I've got good news."

That's what a priest is: a go-between who gets them together. In the Old Testament, Israel was called to be a kingdom of priests; in Exod. 19 we overhear a conversation between God and Moses. God says, "Look, Moses, I could have chosen anybody, but I chose you guys. I didn't have to choose you. The whole world's mine, but I chose you. And I chose you guys to be a kingdom of priests."

And Moses says, "Wow. Is that right?"

Then the Father says, "Go talk to the elders, and get them in line with My will."

Moses goes to the elders with this message: "Elders, guess what. God chose us to be a kingdom of priests."

The elders say, "All that God has spoken, we will do."

Moses runs back to God and reports, "God, I've got great news. We want to do exactly what You asked." Now Israel, from that point on, though they sometimes messed up, were saying, "We want to be a kingdom of priests. We're a go-between."

And God said, "Israel, you are My conduit for Me into the rest of the planet, through My Son, Jesus Christ."

Nobody can imagine what might happen if the laity understood who they are in Jesus Christ.

The Church is in the New Testament what Israel was in the Old Testament. In Rev. 5 and 6, the idea of kingdom of priests keeps coming up. So the role of the contemporary Church is a priesthood. Every person who is in Christ Jesus is a part of the priesthood—a calling to lay ministry. The columnist James Reston said in a Los Angeles press conference several years ago, "Religion is too serious a business to be left to the clergy." William Tanner, former director of the Home Mission Board of the Southern Baptist Convention, underscores the same idea: "I've come to the conclusion that 35,000 Baptist pastors cannot do what God wants done, but 14,000,000 Baptist laity will be able to do it."

Nobody can imagine what might happen if the laity understood who they are in Jesus Christ. Their potential always moves me, especially when I recall Chuck Colson's comment in *The Body:* "The first Christians worshiped God and lived as a holy community, conforming their character to the demands of Christ rather than Caesar. They didn't purpose to turn the first-century world upside down. They did so because of *who* they were" (281). William Gillespie, president of Princeton Theological Seminary and former Presbyterian pastor, said, "The kind of revolution we dream of will only happen if clergy are willing to move over, laity are willing to move up, and all God's people together are willing to move out."

Laity, biblically perceived, are called to ministry. Eddy Hall and Gary Morsch clarify the call issue in *The Lay Ministry Revolution:* "Over the centuries millions of Christians have believed a crippling myth: Ministry is just for 'ministers.' God's call to ministry, so the myth goes, comes only to the select few. The rest of us are laypeople by default, called only to receive ministry and support the ministries of others. However, the Bible renounces this myth with an empowering truth: If I am a Christian, I am called to minister" (16).

Is It *Laikos* or *Laos*?

Two Greek words help unravel our misunderstandings about lay ministry in the church: *laikos* and *laos*. *Laikos* means a layperson who does not understand a particular academic discipline. Much as I say to my medical doctor, "Doctor, I don't understand a word you just said because I'm a layman. Say it again in lay-level language." That is *laikos*. That is where we get the phrase "I'm just a layman." It means one who is not articulate or trained in an academic discipline.

On the contrary, the word *laos* has the rich meaning of "the people of God." The people of God have been especially chosen to make known His wonderful acts. It is intriguing to me that it's the first word, *laikos*, that is used repeatedly in our vernacular today. "Oh, I'm just a layperson," people say, speaking a curse upon themselves that is not true at all according to Scripture.

In the New Testament, the word *laikos* never appears. The rich word *laos* does appear in some of the texts we have already read. It says that the people of God have been especially chosen to make God known.

Yet it is the first word, *laikos,* that is used repeatedly by our people. It's a crippling term. It's a stifling term. It's a word that holds back millions of Christians. It's a tragic word that keeps Christians believing that God uses only preachers and pastors to do His work. The negative consequences for the kingdom of God are alarming and sad. On the contrary, challenging everyone to recognize and act on their call to minister for Christ wins more people, energizes congregations, and gives ministering laypersons a sense of noble satisfaction.

Principle 2—Laity, if They Are Biblically Perceived, Are Gifted for Ministry

At some point during the Middle Ages, the definition for *church* changed into the hierarchy, so where the bishop was, there was the church. That definition of the church ruled out about 97 percent of the people. It was a destructive, false notion. The real Church is where the people of God are—the *laos,* not just the clergy or hierarchy.

The laity are gifted. What do you mean by gifted? God gives every Christian gifts—tools for serving Him that are listed in Rom. 12, 1 Cor. 12, and Eph. 4. Some Bible authorities believe these are exhaustive lists, while others think the lists are merely examples of God's gifting. Either way, the gifts are the abilities or tools God gives every Christian to respond to the call He places on their lives. If I ask one of you to build me a house, and you say, "Yeah, I'll build you a house," and I say, "But you can't use a hammer. You can't use a saw. You can't use a level. And you can't use a square," you would respond, "Without tools I can't build that house." Well, God is not so capricious to ask anybody, including the laity in your church, to do something and then deny them the giftedness for doing what He asks.

Tools and Strategies

Lay ministry, when taken seriously, also helps laypersons say no to ministry that calls for gifts they do not have. At the same time, lay training teaches them to say yes to ministry that calls for gifts they do have.

I am convinced that most burnout in lay ministry is caused by failing to match people's gifts to ministry responsibilities. The tendency among pastors is that they become crisis-driven by situations where someone bails out of a ministry. As pastors, we feel we have to get someone into the vacant assignment quickly, so we recruit the first person we meet rather than starting with a person's gift mix, passion, personality, and temperament. Recruitment should be done much differently.

First determine human resource specifications for a task; then recruit the individual who possesses those gifts. Next you assist him or her into a ministry that uses the gifts possessed.

Temporary Placements

There may be times when somebody steps out of a ministry where the position has to be filled quickly. In that case, you may be forced to recruit someone for a short term who does not have the necessary gifting but with the understanding that the arrangement is temporary. That temporary recruit is not going to feel fulfilled in that area of ministry, nor is he or she going to be very effective.

*I find a recharging
taking place all the time.*

I like to think every Christian has a battery and alternator-generator system built into their ability system. So if you are in a ministry that calls for gifts you have, that battery may be severely drained, but it is being restored and built up by the alternator.

Ministry that uses our unique giftedness may be fatiguing and tough, but it will also be invigorating. Though I never want to do anything else, it is hard at times. There are moments when I wonder, but only for a few seconds at a time. I love what I'm doing. Like many other servants of Christ, I find a recharging taking place all the time.

If you try to do a ministry that calls for gifts you do not have, the battery goes down with no recharging. That person burns out. He or she gets frustrated. So if you have to put somebody in a role that calls for gifts that that one does not have, help the person understand it is temporary.

Understanding Ministry Potentials

A helpful way to free persons from frustration in service is to expose laity to a wide variety of ministries. Beware, pastors; a serious lack of awareness is present on the part of most laity concerning the broad ministry possibilities open to them. So if you ask laypersons what they want to do in ministry, they have a tendency to think, I do not want to change diapers in the nursery, I cannot sing, I do not want to usher, and I cannot teach a Sunday School class. They think almost exclusively of those four fairly visible ministry categories. Beyond that, they cannot think of anything they might be able to do.

A pastor I know preached from Nehemiah on a serious call to lay ministry. He challenged men of his congregation to become more involved. When he gave an invitation, to his shock 75 men came forward to commit themselves to active lay ministry.

Later he was heard to say, "What am I going to do with 75 additional ushers?" That pastor had an extremely narrow understanding of the range of ministry possibilities.

Listen Carefully

Our challenge is to find ways to expose people to the broad arena of ministry. They must also be trained to listen carefully to the directives of the guiding Spirit. They are the people God wants to use.

When she started hearing about lay ministry, a lady in Milwaukee was sure she had no gifts at all. She did not know a thing she could do, and her pastor was not sure she had any gifts. He could not find anything for her to do at church—none of the traditional categories fit her. She looked out her apartment window and saw people standing at a bus stop in the cold. It occurred to her that she could offer them coffee. So she made coffee, took it down, and served it. They asked, "How much?" "No charge." "Really, why not?" "Because I am doing this for Jesus; He impressed me to bring you coffee." A person who thought she had no giftedness ministered profoundly in the name of Jesus. As a result, her Master's fame spread across Milwaukee.

Another lady would go to a Laundromat late at night. People were oftentimes frustrated being there so late, but she would come in with fresh-baked cookies. "How much?" "Nothing. I'm doing this in the name of Jesus."

Many Churches Have Hundreds of Opportunities

The list keeps growing if we expose our people to the broad possibilities of ministry. Many of them are amazed to discover how many ministry opportunities are available in every church. In fact, the number might surprise even a senior pastor.

When I was on staff at Bethany First Nazarene in Bethany, Oklahoma, my assignment was minister of lay development, but I actually ran a job placement bureau for the church. I did hundreds of interviews, trained others to do the same, and then placed individuals into ministries in the church.

As a foundation for that ministry, I made a complete list of all ministries in that church. I discovered the list was amazing and spiritually challenging. The worship attendance was around 2,000 at that time. We were absolutely shocked to identify 1,471

weekly ministries. Most people had no idea how many opportunities there were to use their giftedness. Try making a complete
list for your church. You will be surprised how many ministries
your church offers, how many different gifts are needed, and
how many gifts your people possess.

At Skyline Wesleyan Church, we have a Ministry Opportunity Sheet that lists 3,507 ministries. This is a traditional list,
and you can find far more things that can be done in the name of
Jesus in your church. Exposing believers to the wide arena of
ministry is critical to helping them understand their own giftedness and their need to serve.

Share the Challenge

I am convinced the main reason so many parachurch ministries attract the cream of the personnel crop is because they
present people with a big challenge. Some people are undermoti-
vated by the normal opportunities of ministry in a local church
because they do not know of needs and possibilities. That's the
reason Bill Bright comes through town and gathers many top
givers around him because he says, "If I had $1 billion, I could
reach the entire globe with the gospel of Jesus Christ." So people
write out checks wanting to win the world.

The dreams of many churches are too small. Their vision is
not city focused or county focused. They have no strategy to
reach a whole area. Remember, vision attracts money. Vision attracts people. Ministry hours flow to vision. And vision is always
the first step toward mission accomplishment.

With so many working women, the number of available lay
ministry hours has shrunk enormously. In an average week, an
individual in your church is only able to commit an hour or two
to church ministries. But even with the decline in available
hours, people still rally around a vision.

This excitement for vision was demonstrated when I served
on staff at a megachurch in Oklahoma City. Those of us on staff
worked in youth, music, and children's ministries. But we always
had a difficult time getting workers. Why? Because one ministry
in the church had everybody lined up to volunteer for it. That
program had a two-year waiting list of volunteers. The rest of us
would try to get people to serve, but they would say, "Oh, no,

I'm on Brother Sam's list, and I'm going right in as soon as he calls. I don't want to miss my opportunity." Brother Sam oversaw the senior adult ministry and made it so exciting that everybody, even those in their 20s and 30s and 40s, could not wait to work with the senior adult ministry. Vision draws adherents.

Flavil Yeakley, who ministers in the Church of Christ, finished his doctorate with a focus on analyzing lay ministry training. He discovered a pattern about the connection between lay ministry opportunity and church growth. He said there are approximately 60 identifiable weekly ministry positions for every 100 attenders in growing churches. In plateaued churches, there

E xposure to opportunities for ministry has a direct bearing on people serving the Lord and on church growth.

are about 40 identifiable weekly ministries for every 100 attenders. In declining churches, there are only about 27 weekly identifiable ministries for every 100 attenders. His conclusion—exposure to opportunities for ministry has a direct bearing on people serving the Lord and on church growth.

More and More Professional Staff?

The constant temptation as a church grows is to hire more and more staff. Our great challenge, however, is to learn how to develop the staff we have and show them how to mobilize laity for service. They are to produce an army of people who do ministry. It intrigues me that in the Council of Seville, all the way back in the year 619, they said that laity and pastors should be kept separate, and the rationale for this was based on Deut. 22:10: "You shall not plow with an ox and a donkey together" (NASB). Based on that text, they wanted clergy and laity to be kept separate. (I have always wondered in this analogy whether clergy or laity was the donkey!)

As we have seen, everybody has been given different gifts for ministry, but everybody has been given at least one gift that

God wants used. His plan is not for every individual to meet every kind of need. Rather, God plans that all of us working together can meet every need. The great news—or is it the hilarious news—is that God has placed within the Body of Christ all the spiritual gifts needed to minister to the many needs within that congregation and in the world around them.

Mark down two clear-as-day facts: (1) Everybody is gifted to accomplish some ministry; and (2) thousands of Christians are idle because they have never been shown all the possible ministry opportunities in church and society. Let's share these realities over and over with the people of God until everyone joins the lay ministry revolution.

I especially love this crystal-clear summary about gifts and their usefulness from Eddy Hall and Gary Morsch in *The Lay Ministry Revolution:* "As we respond in compassion to needs God brings across our paths, our gifts become active. As we name our gifts, our ministries take on clearer focus. As we find the point where the world's deep pain and our deep joy intersect, we discover our callings. And as we join with others who share our callings and whose gifts complement ours, we are forged into ministry teams through which God's power and love can flow to heal a hurting world" (73).

PRINCIPLE 3—LAITY, IF THEY ARE BIBLICALLY PERCEIVED, ARE TO BE TRAINED FOR MINISTRY

God plans for His Church to be an equipping center. It is intended to be a miniseminary. A few years ago, I received a letter from a Southern Baptist church in Greenville, Texas. Their letterhead read: "Ministers: The people of the church." Then it had a category titled the Equippers of the Ministers, where the names of church staff were listed. They had the biblical pattern printed on the letterhead of the church.

Whose Job Is Ministry?

Dr. Ken Van Wyke, who formerly served on staff at Crystal Cathedral, did a dissertation on Understanding Lay Ministry Training. In his survey, he asked this question of laity: Whose job is it to do ministry? Here were the choices: (1) It's the pastor's job. (2) It's the pastor's job, but he just can't do it all, so we help him do his job. (3) It's a shared ministry. What do you suggest the majority selected? They chose No. 2 overwhelmingly. They clearly showed a gross misunderstanding of the nature of the church—their ecclesiology was grossly dysfunctional. Such an understanding of church by lay members has to change so they view ministry as something all people of God do and share.

I am convinced that some of our vocabulary and some of our systems deactivate laity in service to Christ. We talk about how many our buildings seat, about how many members we have, and about how many attend our services. But that is largely a "passive" number, not active. We even enjoy talking about our church's income, even the number of tithers. All of this may be interesting, but it does not tell us how many mobilized laypersons for ministry for Christ we have.

And we have many people who say about themselves, "I'm *just* a layman or a laywoman." They must be taught that the majority of persons who make up the church are laypersons. They must be taught that the phrase "just a layperson" undermines their value to the cause of Christ and allows them to be passive. It is even possible for them to have perfect attendance at church and still be passive and uninvolved in Christ's mission through the church.

More than "Mess Hall" Mentality

To change, confront, or revolutionize these concepts, lay training is essential. The training I have in mind involves formal instruction, but it involves much more. It must be training that activates good, faithful, regular attenders into active ministers. One person said it this way, "In the military, we give commendation and medals to those who almost lost their lives in battle; but in the church, we give a Purple Heart if people show up on Sunday at the mess hall between 11 A.M. and noon." It's true in too many settings—believers just show up to be fed but seldom expect to work or witness.

But most Christians are not lazy or AWOL or apathetic—rather they just do not understand the call, responsibilities, and privileges of lay ministry. Many have never heard of giftedness and have no idea what their spiritual gifts are. Let me ask you a question: If military personnel just showed up for meals without training for war and defense of their country, would you feel secure, knowing they did not know how to fight the war or fly the planes or drive the tanks? Of course you would not feel secure. Military personnel have to be trained—in fact, they eat so they can train and become proficient at their duties. So it is with the army of the Lord.

Infiltrating the Pagan Pool

To state it another way, how many have been trained and mobilized to be plainclothes persons in the Jesus revolution? Who knows how to infiltrate the pagan pool of humanity with the contagious gospel of Jesus Christ? That number matters much more than how many attend, how many join, and how much they gave in the offering.

Strange as it sounds, we train about 1 percent of the Christian workforce. Generally we train pastors well, and we are rightly proud of a trained clergy. Pastors have degrees, read books, study every week, and participate in training seminars. But the other 99 percent of the church's workforce, commonly called the laity, are largely untrained.

The training they need may involve classes and reading assignments. However, many believers have taken lots of classes but do little or no lay ministry. The training I have in mind goes beyond classes. They need on-the-job training. They need motivation. They need to be taught what Scripture says about their ministry. Training requires a general orientation about the mission and direction of your specific church. Training and equipping mean being sure the laity have identified and sharpened their God-given gifts and possess enough spiritual strength to carry them through tough times.

Models for training are nearly as plentiful as churches. Some are academic models. Some are relational models. Some are shared-on-the-job models. Some are formal-study-and-get-a-certificate models. At Skyline Wesleyan, we have launched what we call Next Level Living, a four-stage strategy for training based on: (1) *experiencing* His love, (2) *knowing* His way, (3) *being* His person, (4) *doing* His work. (Feel free to contact our church if you want samples of this material or go to my web site: <www.jimgarlow.com>.)

Site for Training

Those who have read Elton Trueblood will remember that he thought every church should be a miniseminary so laypersons could be trained for ministry. That discussion is fleshed out in his books *Company of the Committed* and *The Incendiary Fellowship*. Whatever your model, train and equip the laity for ministry.

R. Paul Stevens in *Liberating the Laity* offers these convincing sentences about the most effective site for training: "The best structure for equipping every Christian is already in place. It predates the seminary and the weekend seminar and will outlast both. In the New Testament, no other nurturing and equipping agency is offered other than the local church. In the New Testament church, as in the ministry of Jesus, people learned in the furnace of life, in a relational, living, working and ministering context" (46).

Later Stevens gives seven reasons for his conviction that the local church is where training should be done. For him, the local church is an ideal place for training and equipping laypersons for ministry for these reasons:

1. Scripture assumes the local church is the context for growing to maturity in Christ.
2. The local church is relational and thus provides a dynamic environment for learning.
3. The local church has a rhythm related to life that connects learning with living.
4. Local churches have the spiritual gifts needed to do the ministry God wants done there.
5. The local church is multigenerational and provides the family of God a learning lab.
6. The local church knows the character of each person it equips.
7. The local church has a long-term relationship so the training need not be hurried (47-48).

Over and over throughout this chapter, I use the word *training* as if it is a synonym for *equipping*. Without question, equipping involves training, but it requires more. By equipping I mean helping laypersons identify and develop their gifts, but I also mean teaching them to rely on the enablement and empowerment of the Holy Spirit. That enablement seldom comes to either layperson or minister until one gives his or her best and then trusts the Lord for the rest. And it always has to have a high motivation content—to please the Lord.

One common ingredient that was always present in high-functioning laity churches: a sense of excitement about doing Christ's work.

Ken Van Wyke discovered still another fact about equipping and training when he tried to identify the one common ingredient present in what he called high-functioning laity churches that is absent in low-functioning laity churches. I thought he would discover that in the high-functioning laity churches, there was a tremendous emphasis on training classes. He thought, as I did, that churches with low-functioning laity would always be short on classes. It did not turn out that way. A number of high-functioning laity churches had little structural training. And some low-functioning laity churches offered many classes, but nothing was happening. Surprisingly, he found the one common ingredient that was always present in high-functioning laity churches and always absent in low-functioning laity churches. *It was a sense of excitement about doing Christ's work that flowed through the entire congregation.* Evidently equipping and mobilizing have much to do with atmosphere and pulpit teaching. They have to do with giving permission for lay ministry. The effective churches had a clear mission. They had an understandable purpose. They knew exactly why their church existed and were excited to be a part of what God wanted to do through their congregation.

Training Is More than Books and Classes

While serving as pastor of Metroplex Church in Texas, I stopped in the 7-Eleven store and was filling my car with gas early one Sunday morning. I was struggling to get my eyes open, pumping gas, and frustrated with myself for not getting gas the night before. All of a sudden, I heard an invitation in a strong Hispanic accent: "You've got to go to church with me." It was loud, almost irritating. I looked up, and there was this man in my face, pumping gas right on the other side of the pump. He said it again, "You've got to go to church with me." I said, "Pardon?" Standing beside his old, brown, beat-up pickup, he repeated his invitation, "You've got to go to church with me this morning." I said, "Why is that?" He said, "Because Jesus will be there!" Now he had my attention. I said, "Wow, that's great." He was aggressive. I said, "I love your excitement, but I'm a pastor of another church, and I'm on my way there now."

I thought he would say something like, "Oh, blessings on you, Pastor." Instead he said, "Makes no difference. Come with me. *Jesus will be at my church.*" You know what? I really wanted to go. I believed he was absolutely right. I went to my congregation that morning and told them that story. (I did not tell them what church the man attended though!)

As I thought about my meeting with that aggressive gentleman, I prayed, *O Lord, give me 10,000 just like him.* I call it the "beat-up, brown pickup ministry." Lay ministry means sending guys out to 7-Eleven at gas pumps to say, "Come to my church. Jesus is going to be there." If you have to choose between attending training classes and zeal, choose zeal.

Now how many training classes did this guy go through? Probably none. But he had a sense of excitement about doing Christ's work. He was driven by a mission. And you know what, I sometimes attended his church on Sunday nights and never told anybody in my church. It was a live place. Their church had little formal kind of instruction, but their services were so vital that my loud friend just knew he had to tell someone. Do not merely have training classes. Ideally, have well-planned classes *coupled* with such spiritual vigor.

PRINCIPLE 4—LAITY, IF THEY ARE BIBLICALLY PERCEIVED, ARE TO BE SENT INTO MINISTRY

Ministry never occurs in isolation. It happens when we, as members of the Body of Christ—His Church—join our brothers and sisters in a mission to the world. We do not minister as individuals; we minister as members of something much greater than ourselves—the eternal Church of Jesus. Thus, when the *laos* sent a person on a ministry, he or she went out with the support of all who were part of the Church.

Our model of ministry—Jesus himself—was sent into ministry. In His prayer in John 17, Jesus says that He had been sent by God the Father into the world. In a similar way, Jesus sent His followers into ministry: "I sent them into the world, just as you sent me into the world" (v. 18, TEV). On another occasion, Jesus spoke to His disciples: "As the Father has sent me, I am sending you" (20:21).

Being sent into ministry means called, gifted, and trained laypersons are on a divine mission; they have a specific task. As they do this task, they function as representatives of the sending party, the Church.

*he laity have
ambassadorial status from
God through His Church,*

There is a difference between being called and being sent. Charles Lake carefully notes the difference: "Biblically speaking, God's call is not to go somewhere, but to be someone by His grace. It is in His sending that our direction is made known as to the geographical location. . . . He calls us to himself in order that He might send us to others. Such is a very sound biblical principle" (Garlow, *Partners in Ministry,* 138).

Unpacking the word *sent* means credentialed to act as one's representative for the purpose of accomplishing a specified mission. That's the precise issue. Our laity are to be sent into ministry. What are the credentials? They are twofold: (1) the call of God and (2) being sent by the Church. Thus, the laity have ambassadorial status from God through His Church, and they are called to a specific mission: to make known the wonderful acts of our God.

We live in exciting times. We appear to be on the verge of a reclaiming of our biblical heritage that every believer is called to ministry. You are a participant and an active agitator of that revolution. Make it happen in your sphere of influence.

This massive strategy will eventually cause every tongue to confess Christ and every knee to bow to Him in worship. It isn't here yet. I can't quite see it. But I hear distant sounds. Listen with me. Let's believe we are to be the generation to usher in the revolution when *every one of God's children* will say, "I am part of the ministry of Almighty God."

I doubt that Peter Drucker was thinking about lay ministry when he wrote this accurate sentence—"The purpose of a team is to make the strengths of each person effective and his or her weaknesses irrelevant"—but it applies to the church (quoted in Gene Wilkes, *Jesus on Leadership,* 220). Everyone is needed to do lay ministry with the giftedness God has given them.

May a massive revolution of lay ministry occur by laypersons entering ministry as plainclothes agents. A Jesus revolution—the only revolution that will untimately conquer the hearts and minds of humankind!

SECTION II

Develop a Staff to Implement Lay Ministry

▪6▪

MASTER PLAN FOR BUILDING A DREAM TEAM
Develop a Single Heartbeat Staff

Dale E. Galloway

Coach Paul "Bear" Bryant, college football legend, did more than win games. He was a master at bringing the best out in people. He enjoyed telling how he did it: "I'm just a plow-hand from Arkansas, but I've learned how to hold a team together. You have to lift up some, calm others down until you find you have got *one heartbeat together.* That's all it takes to inspire people to win."

One heart beating together—what an inspiring idea for church teams too.

Developing "one heartbeat" may be the most important part of growing an effective church staff. Too many staffs are not a team. Rather, they are isolated individualists or position specialists. Though they may fulfill specific assignments and do their work well, they are not committed with one heart to the whole mission of a church.

DEFINING A WINNING TEAM

You lead a winning staff when all members of the church staff work together to make the shared vision a reality. They become an actual team when they work with "one heartbeat together" to carry out the mission of Christ through your church. That's a good working definition of an effective church staff—a group working together to achieve a common vision of carrying out Christ's mission through a specific congregation.

91

A Team Increases Achievement

Think of staff development as a giant puzzle where you as pastoral leader see a picture of what your church is to become. Then you start to put the right people together to make the puzzle work.

I live in Lexington, Kentucky, which is the heart of Kentucky basketball. The Wildcats under Coach Tubby Smith are a great example of a true team. One year they won the national championship without any known superstar on the team. What an inspiration it is to watch that basketball team come together so they are so much more playing together as a team than they are as individual superstars.

Church staffs must be like that too. Effectiveness starts with building the right team players. Achievement continues as you help them learn to work together. The "fit" is important.

Years ago, a close friend who pastored a large church asked me to help him with his staff. After a few sessions, I recognized that they had some of the finest talent to be found anywhere. My pastor friend had searched the country for prospects and carefully chosen key persons. Each one was well trained and possessed fine credentials. Several had years of experience. But as I dialogued with them individually and as a group, I realized each person was doing his own ministry in a kind of friendly isolation. As a result, their effectiveness was fragmented. They were a group of good people but far from being a team.

*Everyone achieves
more on a "one heartbeat
together" team.*

When I returned to our New Hope Community Church staff, I felt a wonderful new appreciation for them. Our people were not nearly as well talented, nor did they have the professional reputations of the other staff. Many of our team were homegrown, developed out of lay ministry in our own congregation. But I thanked God for them because we worked together with a sense of oneness, vision, and mission. We sincerely cared for one another.

Our team commitment at New Hope was so much more evident than what I experienced among the other staff. Authentic staff teams can build great churches, but a thousand specialists who do not share a common vision will never do it.

At New Hope, we held three church growth conferences each year as a service to other churches who wanted to learn from us. These conferences required an extra-mile effort from our staff, but it was always encouraging to hear remarks like, "Your staff loves each other. We see you enjoying each other's friendship. Our staff is not like that."

A team like ours was worth every effort in staff development. Everyone achieves more on a "one heartbeat together" team. Meanwhile, all members of the team experience greater satisfaction in their own efforts for Christ.

Recruiting and Developing Staff

Finding or growing staff members requires serious intentionality and divine guidance. It demands that a pastor understand his or her leadership style. For maximum results, the senior pastor must use methods of training, supervision, and accountability that develop people and strengthen the sense of team commitment.

Building a staff team is one of the senior pastor's most important challenges. Teams have such great potential to multiply your church's ministry to more people. This is why the senior pastor has to focus on staff development. When done well, the possible impact is beyond measure. When staff development is done poorly or neglected, the church suffers and staff persons become frustrated, unproductive, negative in their attitudes, and eager to move to another assignment.

One important rule—never hire a staff member just because it is convenient. I have done that, which is a big mistake. Never add someone because you feel sorry for him or her. It is so easy for pastors to let compassion override their sound judgment. So they hire people who are out of a job because they failed in their last assignment. Please realize that those people will probably fail again—probably in your church if you hire them for your team.

Sometimes pastors bring on good, well-trained people without adequate thought about how they fit the vision for the whole church. That, too, can cause problems. Before a new staffer is added, try to envision how their uniqueness fits your situation. Give careful consideration to how each prospective staff member fits on the team.

As you recruit staff, think through what kind of a person you need. Do you need a maintenance or producer type? If you have only enough funding for one person, who would that be? What talents are you looking for? What would the specific assignment be? Would you hire a maintenance ministry person to take care of the elderly—a chaplain type? Or would you hire somebody to win new people to Christ? When you hire a producer type, you usually win more people, your church grows more, you receive more funds, and you can soon add another staff person.

On the contrary, adding a maintenance type person might produce a deeper, more solid ministry to an existing group. Though a church may need both producers and maintenance type staffers, both do not contribute equally to fulfilling your vision for the congregation.

Staff recruitment and development almost always creates some frustration. Expect it. One thing that can nearly drive a senior pastor crazy is getting one ministry working well, and then realizing something has gone wrong in another ministry.

It sounds so wonderful to have a 15- to 20-person staff. But when you have that size staff, there is never a time that 2 or 3 are not in some difficulty or that you have at least 1 opening.

It was a standing joke at New Hope that I could never take a vacation without the resignation of a staff member or the development of a serious personnel problem. Recruiting, developing, and nurturing a staff requires hard work that demands constant commitment and forgiving grace. At the same time, the combined achievements of a "one heartbeat together" team makes every effort worthwhile.

One of the most critical points in staff development is adding the first person. He or she often sets the pattern for future staffing in that congregation. Therefore, it must be done well to meet immediate as well as future needs.

In one-pastor churches, the first staff person is often added without much thought about the individual "fit" to the congregation. The idea is a kind of let's-find-a-live-body-and-let-him-or-

> *I t is important that a pastor consider staff recruitment and development to be among the most significant work he or she will ever do.*

her-go-to-work mentality. Resist that temptation and be especially careful about the first staff person you add. The wrong person can destroy your ministry or set back the church's willingness to work with staff. A bad choice also hinders a congregation's willingness to add other staff members. Thus, it is important that a pastor consider staff recruitment and development to be among the most significant work he or she will ever do.

Develop a Master Plan

I passionately urge every pastor to think, plan, develop, and write the master plan of what God wants to do through your ministry in the present setting. First, develop a vision, and then create a master plan to make the vision a reality. Then add only those staff people who fit the master plan.

Staff personnel, no matter how talented or experienced, who do not share the vision and commit to the master plan will quickly become serious liabilities. Such persons use up a pastor's physical and emotional energies in a negative, dead-end way.

For instance, suppose a core value in your master plan is that lost people really matter to God. Then if you add a staff person who only wants to nurture established believers, you will never have the same heartbeat.

Use Pastoral Authority

To build a great church, it is absolutely necessary that the senior pastor have authority to hire and fire personnel. We put this into the bylaws at New Hope almost by accident. I was 31 years of age, dreaming the great New Hope dream of launching a church without any people. As a kind of informal research for those start-up days, I wrote several churches, asking for a copy of their bylaws.

In the process, I received Dr. Robert Schuller's bylaws from Garden Grove Community Church, now known as the Crystal Cathedral. I copied word for word from his bylaws the part that indicates the senior pastor has authority to hire and fire staff. I did not realize how important that authority was until the church started to grow and we added more staff. The more staff we added, the more important that authority was.

Here's how to work this principle: If everyone—staff members, lay leaders, and congregation—knows the senior pastor has this authority, it settles many issues before they come up. In Portland, the staff reported to me, and I reported to the board for the whole team. That meant I was responsible for the staff on a daily basis. It meant I possessed an overall awareness of what every staff member was doing.

If you don't already have that authority, there are several ways to establish it. For example, if you have a pastor-parish relationship team or personnel committee, you need to work closely with it, influencing the members to nominate the people you think would work best with your style and vision for ministry. One Methodist pastor I know makes time for a monthly breakfast with the man who chairs the committee. Beyond that he is very intentional about bringing people onto that committee who recognize his leadership role.

Another way is to work through key influencers. I found you can talk about this issue with lay leaders who own or run a business. They understand because no businessperson would want people working in his or her company who are not accountable to the leader. The next step is to encourage those key decision makers to establish such a policy in writing.

Here is the healthy dynamic such authority encourages. It keeps me from hiring someone the church does not want. Neither will I fire someone who is well appreciated. But sometimes staff people have to be asked to resign because they are not effective or because they cause problems on the team.

The driving criteria for every staff member's continued service is God's master plan for your church. Like many other ministry privileges and duties, every senior pastor must view this authority to hire and fire as a trust from God and as a confidence from decision makers in the church. In short, leaders find a way to build the team they can work through to recruit the kind of staff they need.

When the direct line of authority comes through the board to the senior pastor to the staff, everyone—including the board, staff, and congregation—knows who the leader is and who is casting the vision. Then staff members know where to go for guidance. They feel secure in their relationships and fairly treated in their accountability. They know that they will be evaluated by the one who knows the most about their ministry.

> *ou will never build a great team if you are not both the official and informal leader of the staff.*

The dynamics of good staff relationships with the senior pastor's authority reminds me of a special friend who was on our staff for many years. I raised him up in ministry. He was 6 feet, 10 inches tall and amazingly gentle. But I noticed that people respected him wherever we went. He seldom raised his voice, but nobody messed with him.

This issue of senior pastor authority is a lot like that. When everybody knows who has authority, though it is seldom mentioned or used, no one pushes or shoves. On the contrary, when no one knows who has responsibility over staff, chaos easily erupts in a church. Then mass confusion reigns because everyone feels a need to build his or her own power base.

Here's the reality: You will never build a great team if you are not both the official and informal leader of the staff.

CONCEPTS FOR BUILDING A DREAM TEAM

Choose people who share your concepts of ministry but possess gifts and abilities that are complementary to your skills and to the skills of other staff members. But how is that to be accomplished?

Compatible Ministry Philosophy

My philosophy of ministry says a church must offer everybody faith, hope, and love just as Jesus did. I believe if you put faith, hope, and love inside people, they will always come out on top. Then nothing can defeat them. That's positive, biblical inspiration.

Yes, we recognized sin and the negative side of issues, but we always showed people the way to new beginnings. That's a philosophy of ministry with me that permeated everything we did, so I needed staff persons who shared those commitments.

Let me more fully explain the importance of this concept. New Hope Community Church was born out of my brokenness. Out of my own pain, God called me to start a church to heal hurts and rebuild broken dreams. As a result of that focus, our church never had a shortage of people. Fragmented persons came because they felt accepted and cherished.

If a potential staff member did not care about broken people, he or she would not fit our ministry. Nothing wrong with another philosophy of ministry, but it simply did not fit at New Hope.

Keep realistic when looking for staff people. Lots of good people would not fit at New Hope. Lots of good people won't fit on your staff, either. Therefore, you must be very selective in choosing staff members. From the first conversation with prospects, discuss philosophy of ministry.

In the recruitment and interview process, be sure to clearly state—more than once—your philosophy of ministry. Ask the person being considered to articulate their philosophy of ministry. Freely discuss how your two understandings of ministry will fit together. Articulate your philosophy clearly, and show potential staff people how you expect it to work in their assignment.

Ministry vs. Performance

Choose people who are focused on ministry rather than performance. Make sure potential staff members know they are being considered for a ministry, not a position or job.

Years ago, my wife went to a music ministers' conference. She came back with this observation: "You could quickly divide the room into two parts. On one side were musical performers, and on the other side were people who saw church music as a ministry."

Some, but not all, can do both. One of our greatest musicians at New Hope could sing wonderfully as a performer, but she also took us into God's presence. She knew both ministry and performance. Should I be forced to choose, I would take someone who sings as ministry over one who is an artistic performer.

Added Gifts and Talents

Select staff persons for assignments with skills you do not possess. Choose someone who is more capable than you are in some area of ministry. Add people with abilities, talents, and gifts that complement yours and other staff members. If you need a youth pastor, choose someone who knows a lot more about reaching teens than you do. The same applies to children's pastor, music leaders, and other ministries.

Sadly, some pastors feel threatened by capable people. Insecurities hinder the work of God in many churches. Though the influence is subtle, it is unproductive. As a result, weaklings who limit or even undermine the church's development are added. Choosing low-talented people tends to weaken the congregation's confidence in the entire staff. At the same time, it makes thinking people wonder about the senior pastor's abilities to choose and develop staff. Then everyone loses.

Look for the most capable people you can in a particular area of ministry. When an opening comes, try to fill it with a more capable person than the one you lost. Then staff changes always take you higher. When you find those kind of team members, honor them, respect them, encourage their creativity, pay them well, and give them reasons to stay a long time.

After thorough discussion and orientation, staff persons should be assigned an area of ministry and given responsibility, authority, budget, and support. Make sure they have room to grow as persons, and help them feel free to develop their assignment as effectively as they can envision. Give them encouragement and affirmation.

Give Ownership

All effective leaders had someone in their past give them

freedom to achieve. They stretched, and their ministry was better as a result.

Here's how I gave ownership to staff persons. I would say to a new staff person, "Don, this is your area. You dream it. You envision it. Let me know how I can help. Otherwise, it's yours. Does that excite you? I expect you to blow the walls out. Go for it. I am just the coach."

When given ownership and trust, capable people will usually surprise you with their achievement. I try to remember Ralph Waldo Emerson's wise words, "Our chief want is someone who will inspire us to be what we know we could be" (Glenn Van Ekeren, *Words for All Occasions*, 233).

In the beginning stages of growing a church, pastors sometimes make the staffing mistake of putting all their resources into one person. For example, if you can only afford one staff person, you must ask the question, "Can I afford someone who spends full time in music alone? Or youth alone?"

As a rule, a church needs 300 to 500 in attendance before it can afford a specialist over one area. In a smaller growing church, those first staff members have to be more multigifted to be able to serve over many areas. Or they need to be part-timers.

Think what happens if you build staff people who build laity who build ministries.

Start where you are. Though he was not speaking about church, try to follow Theodore Roosevelt's advice: "Do what you can, with what you have, where you are." Staff development is never perfect. It is always a work in process. If you wait to develop staff until everything is just right, you will never do it.

Effective staff achievement usually happens when a pastor believes in staff members, gives them a sense of ownership, trusts them to do good work, and motivates them to grand effort in the worthy name of Jesus.

Hire People Who Will Multiply Others

Think what happens if you build staff people who build laity who build ministries. When we had 6,300 members at New Hope, 80 percent of whom had never before belonged to a church, all 18 staff members had the same No. 1 duty on their job description: "Recruit, train, and build leaders in your area of ministry." As a result, a church's whole ministry multiplies. After a while, an expansive curve begins to work—multiplication times multiplication times multiplication.

On the contrary, if you only bring people on staff who do all the work themselves, it vanishes when they move away or die. The pastor's exciting task is to intentionally build staff people who multiply their ministry through others.

Recruit the Strongest People You Can Find

When looking for a staff member, don't settle for anything less than the best. Always hire upward!

Let's consider Tony (not his real name). When we started New Hope, we did an outside drive-in service for eight years. Predictably, our children's ministry was extremely weak.

Therefore, when we moved into our first multipurpose building, we desperately needed to improve our ministry to kids. I knew Tony taught school and had a master's degree in education, so I put him in charge of children's ministry. I thought he was the right person who could build up this ministry of our church.

Soon 300 kids were coming to Sunday School. Then I would say to Tony, "So-and-so would make a great children's teacher. Why don't you recruit him or her?" Later I learned he had never talked to any of the individuals I suggested. But I would see him in the hallway on Sunday morning, kind of pushing people into these classes to teach.

In two or three weeks, these people would be screaming for help. Chaos reigned. Even my own kids hated Sunday School.

Then I made a discovery about Tony. He recruited downward because he did not feel good about himself as a person. Though he did not understand the problem, it was real. Mark it down: a leader's problem, if it is not resolved, quickly turns into a problem for the whole church.

Soon I recruited a strong woman as our children's pastor who saw the vision of reaching people. She bonded with the New Hope dream. She saw how we could group children in many different ways. She began to recruit the best people she could find.

I finally saw a day when we had 200 people working in children's ministry. Kids were grouped 10 different ways during the week, and a couple thousand kids took part each week. The difference happened because someone recruited straight across and upward instead of downward. It is a fact—a person who does not feel good about himself or herself will frequently self-destruct, sometimes at the moment of his or her greatest success.

Ask yourself this penetrating question: How do you recruit? To be a successful senior pastor or staff person, you have to be a recruiter. Evaluate yourself candidly.

- Who do you recruit?
- Do you recruit downward?
- Do you recruit straight across?
- Do you always stretch to get strong people?

Force yourself to recruit and cherish the most capable people in both staff and volunteer assignments. Strong staff leaders produce more strong lay leaders. Always remember—strong staff members grow effective ministries, and strong staff members do not require as much supervision as weak ones do.

Change and Grow

Every staff member requires you to make some adjustments. Every time a new staff person is added, there will be adjustments for you, for the staff person, for other staff members, for lay decision makers, and for the congregation. Everyone must expect it.

This process is like adopting a new child into a family. The adjustment phase provides a good time to initiate dialogue among the staff and lay volunteers to see how everyone is changing to accept the new staff individual.

To a very large degree, a staff member's acceptance depends on how the senior pastor adjusts and accepts. So much depends on your opening your heart and arms. Staff and congregation will follow your lead on how you view a new leader as a valued team member. Few staff members are ever well received by any congregation without some significant help from the senior pastor.

Specialization and Common Ministries

Think through areas of specialization as well as common ministries for which every staff person has responsibility. Make every effort to communicate assumptions clearly and frequently. Common responsibilities are phases of ministry that cross specialties, like Bible reading, caring for each other, stewardship, and prayer.

An example comes from my first visit to Korea. I came back excited about prayer, so I shared my enthusiasm with the staff. We agreed we wanted to become a praying church. That sounded good to everyone.

Then we asked a lady on our staff, "Would you be our pastor in charge of prayer and build a prayer ministry?" She agreed and went to work.

About six months later, I recognized what had happened. Every time we met, we called on this woman to pray. Without realizing it, the other staff members checked out on prayer because the church had a pastor who specialized in prayer.

So I went back to staff and asked ourselves, "What happened? I confess I am as guilty as anyone, but this is not right. Every one of us must take some responsibility for the prayer life of our church." So we agreed each of us would try to be a model of prayer.

As senior pastor and staff members together, your team must think through these issues of common responsibility and specialized duties. What does every staff person do, and what is one's specialization? For me, I want every person on my staff to be involved in small-group ministry. I want every pastor to recruit and deploy laity. I also want every staff member to model prayer.

ANOTHER SERENDIPITY FOR PASTORS

Here's a review of the principles for developing a dream staff team:

Choose staff who have a compatible ministry philosophy.

Choose people who are ministry centered.

Choose staff who add gifts and talents to the team.

Choose people you trust with ownership.

Choose people who accept your main priority.

Choose the strongest people you can find.

Be prepared to change with every staff member you add.

Communicate the relationship of common ministries and specialties.

That's my heartbeat—to win people, involve them in great Kingdom efforts, and help them mature as Christians. Then a church prospers almost as a serendipity of doing what God wants His church to do.

7

STAFF DEVELOPMENT AT DIFFERENT SIZE LEVELS

How to Develop the Right Team

Jim Jackson

Our assumptions determine how ministry is done under our leadership. All pastors' behavior and reactions are shaped by their assumptions. Interestingly, assumptions may be almost unknown to the minister, and often they have never been critically examined.

Three bedrock assumptions form a solid foundation for staff recruitment, hiring, development, and accountability. These concepts shape everything the minister thinks and every relationship a pastor develops with a staff.

First, teamwork is the way things get done. Teamwork, whether with volunteers or a combination of paid staff and volunteers, is an essential ingredient of effective church life regardless of congregational size. Church staffs do not need "stars" as much as competent persons who are good team players.

Second, effective team leaders blend strengths of team members into a powerful force that is much more productive than the sum of its parts. Thus, a well-led team of 10 can accomplish much more than 10 individuals could do independently. This is Christian service synergism at work.

The third supposition is that every pastor needs a staff. Of course, a staff makes a pastor more productive by multiplied efforts. But there is another seldom discussed issue—having a staff cuts down on injuries pastors so often experience in so many phases of ministry.

Satan loves to attack those who have no support group. Thus, when pastors work alone, their ministry allows too much room for the enemy's attack.

Sending Christian workers one by one to do ministry is unbiblical and nonproductive. Not a shred of New Testament evidence supports sending a person to do ministry singlehandedly. But it is the way we deploy them, and godly pastors are often injured by the practice. Perhaps this one-person practice started as an economic necessity and then grew like a troublesome weed. Many church traditions do it, including Roman Catholics, Greek Orthodox, Evangelicals, and charismatics.

It is the law both of the jungle and the church that a pastor who works alone gets "picked off" by Satan, by the enemy's colaborers, or by good folks who want to make sure the "pastor knows where all the hatchets are buried."

But we can do better. In New Testament times, persons were sent two by two. Though NBA Coach Pat Riley may not have the church in mind when he wrote these words, they are true for all of us in ministry: "Great teamwork is the only way to reach our ultimate moments, to create the breakthroughs that define our careers, to fulfill our lives with a sense of lasting significance" (*The Winner Within*, 15).

When I first became a member of the Northwest Texas Conference of the United Methodist Church, I pastored the great First Methodist congregation in Lubbock. The conference church planting planning group said to me, "We want you to help us start a new church within the geographic area of the conference near your church."

I replied, "Let me do some study. I'd like to know what was done in the past. I'd like to get involved in an informed way."

They said, "That's good. Do your research, and let us know what you find."

When I studied the last 10 churches started in Northwest Texas, I discovered nine pastors had moral or spiritual breakdowns. Several pastors or spouses had an affair. Most left the ministry completely. Only one pastoral family survived unscathed—an uncomfortable low percentage.

In each of those new churches, the discouraging factor could be traced back to a one-by-one start-up. On the contrary, the Bible offers examples of many who accomplished much when they partnered with another Christian worker. Scripture also provides many examples of how seldom persons working alone accomplished much.

To spiritually survive and thrive, you must have people yoked with you to do God's work.

You need a staff team for spiritual support. To spiritually survive and thrive these days in ministry, you must have people yoked with you to do God's work. Strength comes from sharing a worthy task with like-minded people. The ministry is a demanding way of life, and it will especially tax you to your limits if you do not have support systems.

A senior pastor, however, who harnesses collective spirituality and combined skills of a team puts the enemy of our souls on the run. A team can achieve something great for God. At the same time, our churches are enlivened when we build affirming links of heart and hand with those around us.

In his book, *Straight Talk for Monday Morning,* the management writer Allan Cox observed about the cantankerous Israelites of Moses' time, "By coming together, they ended their aimlessness" (193). The church I serve recently helped start a new church in Houston. One important prerequisite was requested—if our congregation was to help fund the new church and send people to help start the congregation—that the staff had to be securely in place before the church started.

That idea was revolutionary to many. But I am glad we insisted. Today that church has grown to over 1,100 attending Sunday worship. To a large measure, that progress resulted from starting with a staff rather than with one person.

When financial resources are too tight to start with a team, why don't we challenge potential staff to sacrifice to serve on a start-up team just as we would in starting one-by-one works. Even as missionaries sacrifice or raise their own support to serve overseas, why not call people to a similar near-at-home commitment.

We really do need each other is a principle of human experience and of Kingdom development. Acknowledge the fact that a team accomplishes more and keeps team members encouraged as laborers together for Christ.

THE IMPACT OF CHURCH SIZE ON STAFFING

The way you do ministry must change as the church grows or as you move from one church to another. I discovered I needed to find new ways to do ministry every time my church increased by 100 to 150 people. That's part of the reason why the staff-parish relations committee has been so important to me. On that committee, I need people who know more than I do and who can help me relearn how to do ministry when growth changes the congregation.

As the church grows, ministries have to be shared, or some aspect of ministry will be left undone. In understanding needed changes in strategies and structures, I find Rick Warren's advice insightful and useful: "While the kind of structure a church has does not *cause* growth, it does control the *rate* and the *size* of the growth. And every church must eventually decide whether it is going to be structured for *control* or structured for *growth*. This is one of the most crucial decisions your church will ever face" (*The Purpose-Driven Church*, 378).

For example, I am a pastor who loves to go to the hospital. I love getting down in the ditch with people and helping them out. I love doing ministry for people with pressing needs. I love being a pastor because that is what the Father called me to be.

So when I started doing ministry, I loved going to the hospital five days a week. Now I have to fight to get there one day a week.

Part of the struggle with developing a staff is how you share ministry that you love to do. When you are the pastor of a small church like my pastorate at Ashburn First Methodist Church in south Georgia, you do everything that is pastoral except music. We had a full-time director of music who was also our organist. We had a full-time secretary-treasurer and a part-time youth director. In a situation like that, the pastor does ministry as a generalist.

Then when I moved to St. Mark's, we had 300 members and grew to more than 1,800 members. That presented a very different challenge. In a medium-range church, the pastor is about a half-time specialist and a half-time generalist. I had a larger staff, and I viewed them as a helpful group who expanded my ministry so we could reach more people.

However, when you serve a medium-sized church, the congregation still expects you to be their pastor. Some things cannot be delegated in a middle-sized church because the congregants will not allow it. In that size church, you cannot bring in a visiting minister. In the mid-sized long-established church, people are very slow to accept delegated ministry.

Therefore, the most important staff decision you can make in a medium-sized church is to add one key staff person with whom you become yoked in ministry. As St. Mark's grew, I added an associate pastor who had gifts I did not have.

Find someone with whom you can team in ministry so neither of you are a threat to each other.

Between the two of us, we felt we could reach anybody. I attracted and related to one kind of people. He reached another group. I preached on Sunday morning, and he supported me. He preached on Sunday night, and I supported him. I could not have survived without him.

When you serve a medium-sized church, find someone with whom you can team in ministry so neither of you are a threat to each other. Then be willing to share responsibilities. Though you are the senior pastor, you must have someone who can really help you, or you will not make it.

In a larger church—like Lubbock First United Methodist Church—my role changed again. I was forced to be an administration specialist. That meant I was no longer able to do some phases of ministry.

In a large church, the senior pastor has authority over staff and strategy. To direct those parts of the church's work, you have to be in the office a larger percentage of the time. It becomes necessary to delegate many tasks. Care must be exercised to make sure all phases of delegated ministry are being accomplished, or congregants become critically dissatisfied, with good reason. I had a difficult time making the transition from a medium-sized church to a large church because I could no longer do some phases of ministry.

I thought it would be easy to move from St. Mark's Church in Columbus, Georgia, to Lubbock, Texas. I reasoned, "I'm ready to do this. I've been the pastor of a growing church that added 600 members a year. We're blowin' and goin'. And Lubbock is not doing as well, so I can easily transition."

How wrong I was. Six months after I arrived, I had no idea how to be the pastor of the larger church. I struggled as I was forced to let go of many things.

Then when you ratchet up to another level with 5,000 members, relationship to staff becomes a different animal again. You are no longer an administration specialist or chief of staff, but pastor-teacher.

For example, at Chapelwood I no longer supervise the staff. I introduced that idea to the staff when I first arrived because I had to keep them from becoming dependent on me. The change was difficult for them at first. For a while, I just quit going to staff meetings. Though I have now come back, I do not lead staff meetings.

As I surveyed this larger assignment, I realized I could do a better job of helping the staff if I became a pastor-teacher. At this point my role with the staff is fixing the gaps. When staff persons need help, I move in beside them and work with them in their area of ministry for a while. That makes a big difference for them and helps keep me connected to the front lines.

In this relationship, I can resolve conflicts. I can mentor. I can spend time with staff members. I can express loving concern about their spiritual health. I can show support for them personally. I can express interest in their spouses and family members. I can encourage their professional development. So I meet staff mostly on a developmental level.

Relating to staff differently in various size churches has been a demanding experience. No one ever told me about this need or how to do it.

In a large church, it is often necessary to have a midmanager. It is sometimes difficult to make that relationship work well because anytime you put someone between the senior pastor and the staff, they fight or even sabotage the manager.

I am finding the level I am on now is tough because I have to be absolutely committed to a middle manager. There is no way for me to supervise the staff adequately and still do all the things I must do in order to move the church forward. The list gets long. Somebody has to meet with key lay leaders. I cannot have others do all the funerals or weddings. It is important for me to have a middle manager.

If you have a midmanager, three basic principles must be followed:

First, the midmanager has to have the total confidence of the pastor and the committee that helps the pastor to supervise the staff.

Second, the pastor has to delegate responsibility for the supervision as well as authority for the midmanager to do the work. Of course, you are delegating something that is tough to surrender. But you must trust them with both responsibility and authority. If you give them responsibility without authority, you set them up for failure.

Third, the midmanager must keep the senior pastor informed of everything. I mean everything. There has to be a high level of communication and trust between the middle manager and the senior pastor.

ADVANTAGES OF SERVING ON A STAFF

In addition to the reality that every pastor and every church needs a staff, several advantages of serving on a staff need to be examined, especially by beginners and inexperienced ministers. Consider the following advantages your church provides for persons in staff assignments.

Stimulation

Generally, ministry done in relationship proves to be more

energizing than ministry done alone. It tends to stretch everyone in the group. It works something like the 12-year-old boy who washes the family car—he always does it faster and better when someone helps him.

A healthy, focused staff creates an accumulation of creative ideas and shared energy. As a result, the church, the leader, and other staffers all discover better and more innovative ways to do their work. They feel strengthened and inspired when they realize others are helping them find ways to do ministry better, ways to fit on the team, and ways to please the Lord. King Solomon of Old Testament fame understood this dynamic of service when he said, "Two are better than one" (Eccles. 4:9, KJV). This group-strength reality is the way Jesus sent His disciples out.

Specialization

A staff assignment in a parish church often provides a wonderful opportunity to learn a specialty or to use a specialty in which one has already been trained. No church will be helped by a specialist like the one Benjamin Franklin wrote about: "Tim was so learned that he could name a horse in nine languages; so ignorant that he bought a cow to ride on." Care must be taken to be sure a staff specialist is competent in his or her field of responsibility, loves people, and knows Scripture.

Generalists are becoming a dying breed in the church. Some believe the era of the minister generalist is about over. Often the senior pastor is the only generalist on staff. Specialists for age-groups and special interests have been added in fields like evangelism, pastoral care, administration, and music. But the senior pastor often has to show specialists how their work fits into the whole. Sometimes this process seems like convincing engineers and mechanics how much they need each other.

Staff assignments allow leaders to specialize in areas of their gifts, talents, and strengths. As a result, a congregation has less expectation that every staff person can and should do everything.

The two Ds apply—staff members have opportunity to develop the gifts God has given them and to deploy those gifts. Throughout Christendom, many people have tried to do many things they did not have gifts to do. That causes low morale and creates an awareness of trying to fill slots rather than matching persons with ministries. Good staffing with specialized assignments changes that. So the church is served with greater efficiency and more breadth when at least some of the staffers are specialists.

Just as the medical profession needs generalists as well as specialists, the church cannot get along without them either. For maximum benefits, a congregation should be trained to understand the strengths of each staff member and the ministries the members and the staff can employ to build the cause of Christ together.

Support

When it works as it is supposed to, church staff members support and strengthen each other, including the senior pastor. We all have times when illness, family issues, or ministry problems prevent us from operating at full capacity. When that happens and a staff person is able to operate at only 60 percent, another colleague steps in and takes up the slack.

Meanwhile, a 60 percent effort would not even touch the need for a minister in a solo assignment. With a staff, it is a little like playing high school football when the guard is hurt—you have the tackle pick up part of the work of the blocker and have the center help too. On a team, you can do that. That is how the support system of a staff team works.

Staff members need caring connections from the senior pastor so they can find inner resources for doing their ministries effectively.

A support system also works well when a staffer faces confusion or crisis. In ministry, we all have times when we do not know what the next step should be—that's when staffers are available to talk it over. Scripture calls it iron sharpening iron (see Prov. 27:17).

Another affirming function of the support system occurs when staff members see their relationships to each other as a microcosm of the church. As these persons become an authentic church to each other, healing, hope, and blessing come to them. Then the congregation knows from observation what the church is supposed to be and do. I like to think of this support system as the relationship Jesus had with His disciples. Though the disciples did their part to serve the masses, knowing they were loved by Jesus kept them united. He taught them. He fed them. He healed them. He made himself available to them.

Staff members need caring connections from the senior pastor and other staff members so they can find inner resources for doing their ministries effectively. Such caring seldom develops unless the senior pastor views building relationships and training as an effective way to get people together, to strengthen weak spots, and to become the church within the church.

Mentoring and Professional Growth

Serving on a church staff provides wonderful opportunities to grow professionally and to learn to do ministry more effectively. It provides on-the-job training, much different from any other kind of ministerial training. It is one of the best ways to learn how to pastor a great church. If a staffer dreams of pastoring a growing, vital church, serving as an understudy to the leader of that kind of church is an effective way to learn.

Let's make the application more specific.

The staff person gets to see a growing church at its heart. Of course, professional growth in staff functions operates best when each one has a caring mentor. Quality mentoring only takes place when a senior pastor or another veteran staff member intentionally takes time to develop the less experienced person.

That possibility is not always true of an associate pastor. Too often the associate does only what the senior pastor does not want to do. One of my pastor friends says the only thing worse than being an associate pastor is having one. His observation contains an element of truth.

A young associate is working with me, and is he sharp. He graduated from college with a 4.0 GPA, was a Rhodes Scholar finalist, and was a varsity wrestler in college. He has ability to do almost anything and potential for becoming a great pastor.

The challenge for me is to be such an effective mentor that

he learns everything I can teach him about ministry. Then when he leaves to earn his Ph.D. at Oxford, he can look back on these years as times of spiritual and professional preparation.

One of the most satisfying aspects of being a senior pastor is nurturing staff spiritual development and ministry competence. That makes your church a school in ministry for all who serve with you, gives opportunity for them to teach you, and fulfills your need to pass your ministry to the next generation.

PRINCIPLES FOR HIRING THE RIGHT TEAMMATES

The hardest but most rewarding responsibility a pastor faces is the task of building a staff. Sixty percent of a pastor's success in a middle- to large-sized church depends on your developing an effective team. Locating them and supervising them depends on the senior pastor. Of course, putting the right team together improves ministry to church members—that's important.

But beyond the impact to members, when the right combination of staff are brought together, their new sense of ownership, their positive loyalty, their increased togetherness, and their we-can-do-it attitude will surprise and inspire you. In many ways, such a well-built, well-run staff becomes self-perpetuating and self-renewing. Then though individuals come and go over the years, this healthy contagious spirit continues, often for years.

In one sense, a senior pastor is always on a talent hunt. They are constantly on the lookout both inside and outside the congregation. Some pastors even have a good idea of who they would try to recruit for every assignment if a vacancy should happen. The following are eight important principles to use when you are trying to select the right people for your staff.

I try never to consider a potential staff person if he or she is not capable of one day becoming senior pastor of this church.

Hire the Strongest Available People

You can tell a lot about a senior pastor by the quality of staff he or she recruits. Strong people want a strong staff. Strong pastors plus strong staff members attract strong church members.

Meanwhile, weak or insecure leaders surround themselves with inadequate people because they feel intimidated by strong staff members. The result is often a weak church made up of anemic Christians. I have a pastor friend whose church is sinking more and more each year because he is surrounded with mushy incompetence. There are no quality people around him. The situation is sad, and the congregation gets smaller every year. Regrettably, he blames everyone but himself.

My rule of thumb for choosing associate pastors is this: I never consider a person unless he or she is capable of one day becoming the senior pastor of my church. If one day they could not do better than I, we cannot use them. I need strong, quality people.

So do you. Remember—slipshod recruitment and careless staff hiring finally result in a mediocre church.

Hire Only Equippers

Most church staffs need fewer doers and more equippers. If you hire only doers for major ministry staff assignments, they will accomplish only what one person can do. That is, their achievement will be limited to their own time, energy, and stamina. On the contrary, equippers multiply ministry because they are continually helping others learn how to do it better.

So they try never to do themselves what volunteers can do. In the process, they geometrically multiply ministry and increase a church's ability to serve a growing number of persons.

Equipping is important in any size church, but as a church grows larger, recruiting volunteers becomes harder and harder. So if the staff is not purposely equipping more and more volunteer workers, you will feel pressured to keep adding doers. Soon the staff will get so big and expensive that the church will be hampered rather than helped. At the same time, when potential volunteers are not recruited, trained, and assigned, they miss the blessings Christian service provides. Both of these problems—oversized staff and missed service opportunities—eventually hurt a church's ministry. Both problems can be vastly improved by a staff of equippers who train others to discover and use their gifts.

Don't Hire Based on What You Can "Afford"

Hiring only the most capable people generally costs more money than adding mediocre people, but not as much more as you might think. Generally, if you hire capable persons, they soon pay their own salary by those they attract to your church. If they live nearby, they often bring friends and colleagues who also help almost immediately with additional financial support.

Another return is slower but even more effective—the higher quality of persons attracted to your church by the capable new staffer's ministry. Parents and grandparents are usually more than willing to help fund first-class, competent personnel to minister to families. Sometimes new families with young people appear about the time you add a staff member because they are worried the church they have been attending will not help them keep their children in the faith.

The exact opposite also happens. Over time, you create a negative response by adding mediocre or incompetent people. When those you add are not able to attract people, some of the settled people get restless and sometimes move to another church. So if you start with only what you can afford, you may seriously compromise your church's future. Often adding the right staff member at the right time becomes a significant growth factor in a church, especially if that staffer's area of ministry has been neglected for some time.

Don't Just Fill a Position

Some leaders get panicky if they do not have a vacancy filled in a short period of time. My advice is to make as many people as possible aware of the opening. Consult extensively. Then trust God to lead you to the exact person you need.

Resist your feelings of compassion when hiring staff persons. As pastors, we sometimes feel obligated to help the "underdog," so we hire any live body regardless of that one's record, skills, and emotional strengths.

The problem is greatly increased when you have decision makers on your committees who think the church ought to be an unemployment service where character flaws can be corrected. That reasoning goes like this: "They could get help by working at the church, and we are supposed to help people—right?"

Remember, the blind do not do well in leading the blind; neither do broken people do well in leading other broken people.

If someone needs help, offer him or her help, but do not offer a job. The church always suffers when you hire people because you feel sorry for them. The needy person will also be hurt because the work will be too much for him or her. You will suffer because you will be faced with supervising someone who cannot do the work.

Hire the Best

When you find the right person, you may have to use them for a while outside the position you eventually want them to fill.

There have been times when I hired people because of their gifts when I did not know how I could afford them. Whenever I am able to make connection with somebody I especially need, I do everything I can to reach out and add them to our team. Since competent, capable, committed people are always hard to find, hiring the right people must often take precedence over position.

Clarify Needed Characteristics

Start with a job description and an evaluation of personal characteristics. That will help you, as well as the prospect, get a clearer picture of the exact kind of person needed in your church.

Start your conversation with a prospective staffer by using a job description. Customizing the job description may become necessary as you consider a specific person. But the interview process always goes better if some guidance for discussion, like a job description, is provided. The old preacher was right, "You can always fix something, but it is hard to fix nothing."

The potential staff persons need to know what you expect of them. And you need to be clear on what you will be doing with them in relationship to their assignment. A job description helps develop accurate understandings.

Allowing present staff members to help write the job description for a new person tends to increase unity in your staff, sharpens your perspective of what they are really doing, and triggers a commitment from them to help a new staffer get started well in his or her assignment.

An effective job description for staff members must include at least three things: (1) responsibilities they will have, (2) relationships they will enjoy, and (3) personal talents they need to fulfill the assignment. Strained relationships among staff members and less competence in a staff leader than in the laypersons they lead are some of the largest hindering issues in staff ministry.

In addition to job description, there are other important intangible characteristics a pastor needs to consider in hiring staff personnel: (1) Do you trust their character? (2) How do they deal with money, sex, and power? (3) Do they fit in with other staff members theologically and relationally? (4) Do they share the values of the church? (5) Do they have a healthy homelife? (6) Do they have conflict resolution skills? (7) Will they be loyal to your vision? (8) Is this a person you would want to be a pastor to your family members?

Trust Your Intuitions

The Holy Spirit's part in the process of building a great staff is something we sometimes forget or ignore. Open yourself to what God wants you to do. I have always believed God gives Christians three internal signal lights. The Spirit gives us a red light, a green light, and a yellow light. We do not make nearly as many mistakes when we check which light is shining in our spirit. It is when we run through caution lights that we get into trouble.

I've done that. I am embarrassed by terrible errors I made by not listening more accurately. I believe one of the most significant spiritual gifts a senior pastor has is discerning the spirits. If you ask me which spiritual gift is most needed, I will reply with a scriptural passage. Solomon gave us great satisfaction with his response to God's question, "What do you want? You can have anything," when he said, "I've got to be able to discern" (see 2 Chron. 1:7-10). Perhaps every leader should ask God for that gift.

Take Time to Do It Right

It is usually better to have nobody than to add the wrong person to your staff. It is a little like getting married after two dates—it might work, but it is risky to choose the wrong person. Adding the wrong person to a church staff can create a terrible crisis or long-term mediocrity.

Though many think of the church as a business, it is not a business and never will be. It is a family and a fellowship. I have recently lived through the tension of letting someone go, and I have major scars from the experience. It all started with a big mistake in the hiring process. I moved too quickly, without enough information, and disregarded the yellow light I was feeling inside. Do not make the same mistake I made.

=8=

HOME GROWING YOUR STAFF
Advantages and Disadvantages
of Hiring from Within

Dale E. Galloway

Money and availability of the right person at the right time are the biggest staff development challenges in growing a great church. Money does not buy ministry, and qualified potential staff persons are never easy to find. Overcoming these issues stands at the center of conversation wherever senior pastors meet.

Pastors dream aloud, "If only our church had more financial resources, we could hire more people to help us offer the kind of need-meeting ministry we dream about." Though it is a common belief that money buys ministry, it doesn't. Money only makes it possible for effective people to give time to ministry. But to simply pay more money and to add additional people does not automatically produce effective ministry.

Every church has limited resources. Even break-through churches with large budgets struggle because money and other resources always run far short of perceived need. Few pastors ever have enough financial or personnel resources.

As a result, no matter what size church you pastor or what kind of geographical area you serve, you will never be able to hire enough staff to carry on all the ministries. The needs are too great, the funds too limited, and the talent pool too small. But an alternative solution is available: multiply your resources. Any church can multiply its resources by growing laypeople into ministers; some can even be grown into staff members.

If during my first 10 years at New Hope Community Church you asked me, "Where is the best place to get staff?" my answer would always have been, "Raise up your staff from within your church—that's assuming your church's lay ministry is strong enough to grow lay leaders. My advice: home-grow your staff."

Later in my years at New Hope, I moderated my position so I sometimes hired trained specialists for specific needs. But I have never completely given up the idea of developing the larger part of every church's staff from within the congregation.

Whether persons volunteer service or are recruited, a pastor should think through in advance the advantages and disadvantages of developing staff from within the congregation. Let me suggest several advantages, and you may wish to add your own.

ADVANTAGES OF HOME GROWING A STAFF

Talent Pool Factor

Many laypersons dream about someday being involved in meaningful ministry. They want their lives to count for more than climbing a corporate ladder. Your congregation, in all likelihood, already has several fine men and women who would be willing to devote a major portion of their lives to ministry if you encourage them, if you give them appropriate responsibility, and if you train them for effectiveness. They may be businesspeople who can take time away from their business, early retirees, young adults who give a year or two before they marry, or persons who have always felt called but could never figure a way to answer that call.

I recently met a person like that. She was a widow, newly retired after 20 years as a successful high school principal. She excelled in relational skills and possessed a proven record of running a large city high school. After retirement at 55, she volunteered for full-time service through the church she loved.

Yet when she requested permission to start a small-group ministry, her pastor refused because she "was not trained or credentialed for ministry." Not trained? A woman who has run a high school in a large city for 20 years. What a jewel. What a rich treasure for any church.

If a pastor and church think only in elitist categories, the talents and gifts these persons can bring to ministry will be missed. Many great and gifted people want to do meaningful ministry. They want to do more than serve as an usher, sing in the choir, and sit through endless meetings. They want to work with people, to make a difference, to do hard stuff, and to enjoy some of the satisfactions that come to you from Christian service. They want to invest themselves in Kingdom causes.

Partially Trained Factor

When effective lay ministry works, basic difficulties regarding availability and financial support are often considerably lowered for a church. A lay ministry program offers a personnel pool of nearby people whom you already know—some you know well.

You have the advantage of the observation of their ministry gifts and relationships over months or even years before you ask them to join the staff. That's a great advantage over someone you only know from a résumé and interviews.

On the contrary, when you add staff people from the outside, you do not have the same authentic firsthand understanding of a person's skills and commitments. At New Hope Church the lay pastor program provided three levels of involvement and observation: (1) the beginning level, (2) the full lay pastor level, and (3) the lay pastor leader who led a group and also coached and assisted four or five other groups.

Thus when laypersons joined the staff in a newly developed position or an assignment that someone else had vacated, they had experience and knew at least some of the people. Generally, laity moving to staff were asked to start on a part-time basis until they grew their assignment large enough to justify a full-time salary.

Generally it takes a person from outside about two years to do ministry well enough to pay for themselves. That period from start-up to actual achievement is one reason few persons were invited to join the New Hope staff who were not already active and effective in some phase of the lay pastor program.

Easy Choice Factor

From continuing close contact with lay pastors, selecting potential staff members was comparatively easy. As a person's gifts and leadership were demonstrated through their service as a lay pastor of a small group, we could determine whether they had the important pastoral gifts of caring, loving, winning, and discipling others. It is also possible to observe some intangible gifts for ministry that are hard to evaluate unless one sees a Christian worker in action.

Increased Pastoral Care Factor

As a church grows, providing adequate pastoral care becomes more difficult and demands greater intentionality. Though I believe staffing never frees a senior pastor from Peter's admonition, "Tend the flock of God that is your charge" (1 Pet. 5:2, RSV), adding lay pastors to the staff helped me offer more effective pastoral care to more people, always modeling ministry while teaching others to do ministry.

With lay pastor leaders, I multiplied my care for people 500 times. Though it is impossible for one person to offer personal ministry to 6,000 people, I still had people I cared for personally, but I could rest every night because I knew someone was caring for each individual.

Recognition Factor

Potential staffers from the congregation are known and recognized as loving persons of competence. Even in large congregations, at least some persons have observed or even experienced their ministry at close range. As a result, it is amazing how well church members are willing to accept ministry from lay pastors and from staff members they know.

Competence Factor

In many church constituencies, capable laypeople are looking for meaning. The search is so intense they are willing to work part-time or are even willing to wait for a full-time assignment. Some have enjoyed wonderful success across a lifetime in their profession and business. They are capable and useful. Tap into those people. Many of them do not need much money because of pensions, social security, and/or investments. Sometimes they will even work as a dollar-a-year person. Many of these people bring a richness from their background that could greatly impact other members of your church.

Motivational Factor

Promoting a person from lay pastor to staff ministry creates a feeling of strong motivation for other people serving in lay ministry. When we started growing our staff from within at New Hope, some of us were surprised to discover this process created motivation for other lay pastors. As a result, we learned to celebrate those new assignments; I have attended appreciation dinners where lay leaders would applaud for a long time because one of their own was now going to be on the church staff full-time. Apparently they thought, "Maybe that might happen to me someday." Promoting a person from lay pastor ministry to staff ministry creates high morale. Strong motivation among active lay leaders is not always easy to produce, but it is always easy to enjoy. That's what we did—lay leaders, staff, and congregation.

"Quick-Start" Factor

Many lay leaders have established influence and created on-going ministry in the local church. When you hire insiders, they already have influence that allows them to get a quick start in an ongoing ministry.

Consider how different the start is for strangers. Unless they are unusually gifted, it takes months for them to be accepted by those they are assigned to serve. Their credibility and competence have to be established. It often takes outsiders months and months to find their way into the people's hearts and to locate the city streets.

Ready-Fit Factor

A staff person trained from within is often more centered on the basic fundamental ministries of a particular church than a more professionally trained person can be. Most people aren't asking the kind of questions we discuss in higher academic places. Though I do not mean to devalue seminary training in any way, I believe it is not needed by everyone who serves on a church staff.

Not everyone needs the same training to get started in ministry or to be effective. Homegrown staff tend to be more in touch with the environment around your church and its unique culture. Often their experience in the congregation makes them better understand the everyday needs represented in your church community.

Loyalty to Vision Factor

People hired from within already feel committed to the church's vision and to the senior pastor's philosophy of ministry. It is that vision that first attracted them to this specific church and continues to fuel their desire for deeper involvement. When we started New Hope, my wife's cousin, Jeanie, and her husband, Jerry Schmidt, became some of our closest friends. We often went to each other's house to play Rook. One night while playing that game, I started sharing my dream for New Hope Community Church. Their eyes lit up, and they said in unison, "We want to be a part of it."

When our church met at the drive-in theater, Jerry and I went every Saturday night to hang a sign underneath the movie sign, "Drive-in church here." Jerry was at New Hope from the start. He later became one of our first lay pastors. I soon discovered Jerry had a wonderful way with people. He excelled at getting along with everybody. He was such an attentive listener to people—such a compassionate person. He was really an outstanding leader.

So I gave him on-the-job training, and he was the second person to come on our staff half-time. That was 26 years ago, and he is still one of the finest pastors on that staff today. He does more funerals than all the other pastors combined. We called him "Digger O'Dell"!

The reason he is asked to do so many funerals is that he has ministered to so many people over the years. Everyone has great respect and confidence in him. He has never been to seminary. He is a college graduate in business. I taught him ministry one step at a time. For all our years together, he was a wonderful complement to my ministry.

When anyone did not understand my vision or they became upset with me, guess who they called? They called Jerry Schmidt, and he worked through the issues with them. When you grow a staff from within, look for people like Jerry, and develop them.

Homegrown staffers have to know and embrace the dream. I can't image how your church can have strength and focus if your staff people have different core values than yours. That sometimes happens with imported leaders. Because of longer exposure to your ministry, homegrown staff members are much more likely to share your vision and values.

Less Conflict Factor

Homegrown staff members tend to help form a unified staff with less conflict among themselves than other church staffs. These homegrown folks know the heart of the church. They know the key influencers. And they usually know exactly how to get things done through other people.

Other people sometimes do not understand a pastor's point of view. Some conflict is inevitable because of different perspectives, life experiences, and beliefs about what a church is really supposed to be. I am convinced that the more the staff comes together around the vision and values, the less conflict you will have on the team. The advantage of bringing people on staff out of your church is that they already know the vision and core values. You do not have to teach them because they have already caught it.

That is one reason why I could manage such a large staff at New Hope Community Church. I had so many people on staff that I had grown in ministry who knew exactly what I would say even when I was away. They would say it for me. They would, of course, say it according to their own personality in their own way, but it was the same vision and same values that we shared together in ministry.

Enthusiasm Factor

Homegrown leaders are often filled with enthusiasm because being a staff member gives them opportunities to serve God in a greater way than they have done previously. Their enthusiasm is rooted in having more time to do what they already enjoy doing. Of course, you cannot guarantee anyone's success in ministry, but you can affirm them and encourage them to work smart and hard. That helps create an enthusiasm for various assignments staff members are given.

I remember an epic experience just before New Hope Community Church was started. Someone made an appointment for me with Dr. Robert Schuller, who was to become one of my mentors and friends. He was in Portland and arranged for me to come to his hotel room. He received me cordially and inquired about my dream. I shared my vision for the unchurched thousands in Portland, Oregon, and said, "I'm going to start a church in a drive-in theater." Since he started his church in Garden Grove, California, in a drive-in, I thought he would be excited about my plans.

Instead he said, "Sure is tough, Dale, when you start in a drive-in." We had a wonderful time together, and he prayed for me before we parted. After I left, I felt discouraged for days. It took me several weeks to sort through those feelings. Then I realized I was trying to get somebody to guarantee I would be successful. No one can do that.

You can only provide an opportunity. As the lead pastor I had the wonderful chance to provide a lot of people with opportunities for ministry. But what they did with the opportunity was up to them, and they had the privilege to choose how they did their work.

DISADVANTAGES OF HOME GROWING YOUR STAFF

Some 13 or 14 years into the development of New Hope Church, I realized persons with more advanced training were missing on our staff. I started to understand our church needed at least some staff members with specialized expertise to help develop other staffers.

Specialization Factor

As a congregation expands, persons with specialized skills are needed to train staff members who came from the lay pastor personnel pool. In the early days at New Hope, I trained each layperson we brought onto staff. But a day arrived when I no longer had enough time, nor did I know enough about some specializations, to train them.

That's when I realized some highly trained go-getters were needed to serve as resource people to our staff. Those specialists can come from many fields. I know one church whose main administrator served in the military for 20 years, and after retirement became an excellent administrator of a church. Another church that was heavily into media-driven services picked their media leader from someone who had attended seminary and then become an expert with a major network. Now he uses his communication background in full-time service, training staff members at his church. As staff roles have become more and more specialized in recent years, so has the background training required to enable a church staff to move the congregation to the next step of progress.

Fresh Ideas Factor

A church can become hopelessly ingrown by adding staff only from within—everybody may start to think alike. Home-grown staffers are sometimes limited because of their lack of experiences in other congregations, situations, and settings. Then, too, the nature of their close relationship with the senior pastor may make inside staff persons reluctant to suggest new ideas. Outsiders, however, are much more likely to bring fresh perspective and speak up for new ideas.

Next Step Vision Factor

If you limit yourself to recruiting from within, you can find yourself in need of people with the leadership and long-range sight to take the church to new heights. Chances are, your home-grown staff members have gone only as far in ministry as they have experienced at your church. You might need stronger outside leaders who can take your congregation to greater growth and additional ministries.

When New Hope Church grew to about 3,000, I found myself with six key staff people who could handle about 200 people each. That was when I realized I needed people who could handle 500 or 1,000 persons each. I liked everyone on our staff. We were good friends. I identify with what Bill Hybels says—that it is painful to change, but not to change is a whole lot more painful. So I started adding some staff members from outside the church. Often no staff need to be terminated; the changes can be made as people resign, move away, and/or quit.

The bottom line is that I strongly recommend growing staff from lay ministry to staff positions whenever you have those people in your church. However, when you need more professionally trained persons or those who are advanced in a specialty area, then go out and recruit the best you can find.

GETTING READY TO HIRE FROM WITHIN

Are you are ready to explore the idea that your next staff member might come from within your congregation? Taking these four steps can help you find those God is calling to join you on your staff team.

Establish the Model

In every way possible, model to the congregation that every staff member, including the senior pastor, will always be modeling ministry while teaching it to others. Everyone on staff will be involved, each leading his or her area of responsibility. Each staff member will give strong emphasis to developing others in ministry by having an intentional plan and modeling what they teach.

Build Strong Lay Ministries

If you, the senior pastor, say over and over throughout the congregation and in staff, "Laypeople can pastor," they will believe it. If you make that idea a watchword sentence, your church members will accept pastoral care from their peers. This was one of the keys to our lay pastor ministry that built New Hope Community Church. Growing staff people out of your own ministry begins by building a strong lay pastor ministry. Identify people with pastoral gifts, and put them to work. Remember, not all of the effective people in Scripture had professional training. When Jesus started enlisting the Twelve in ministry, they were fishermen!

Make Heroes of Lay Leaders

Advancing a person from a lay pastor to a paid ministry position helps motivate others to improve their serve. Let them know they are cherished. Underscore in public the importance of what they are doing for the Kingdom. Establish the pattern of inviting effective lay leaders to serve on staff part-time. Then as their ministry grows, they can be added to full-time work.

Hire Only People Who Fit Your Master Plan for Staffing

Look for ministry-centered persons. Make sure they mesh well with the existing ministry team. Hire only people who fit the master plan. And if you do not have a master plan, ask yourself many questions about how these people fit and what they can do effectively. Keep reassuring yourself that those who begin ministry this week will be the leaders of tomorrow's church.

WHEN TO HIRE FROM OUTSIDE

Specific Expertise Is Needed

You should consider hiring from the outside only when you need expertise or a higher level of competence in an area or areas where none exist.

Trainers of Staff

You should consider adding a staff member from the outside when you need someone to offer more advanced training and leadership for the people in that area of ministry. Care should be taken that your staff and volunteer ministers are well trained in their areas of ministry.

Fresh Ideas

An outside staff member is needed when creativity and new ideas run low. I will never forget being in a staff meeting where I felt nobody but me ever had an idea. That's when I knew I needed some new people from outside to bring in fresh ideas. I knew that even though we were growing by 500 to 700 new members per year, which we did for 15 years straight, we needed more new ideas.

Higher Growth and Outreach

Go outside when you need stronger leaders to take your church to higher levels of outreach and growth. Adding one or more outside staff members will often create a higher tide of effort and achievement across the whole staff team.

USING *RATE* TO EVALUATE POTENTIAL STAFF MEMBERS

Whether you are adding staff from within or without, some scale or evaluation is needed to help you know an individual before he or she is added to your staff team. One of my strengths is that as a pastor I always offer people hope. That means I often see possibilities in people that others cannot see. Believing in individuals sometimes motivates them to stretch and grow into successful staff members. But the exact opposite sometimes happens too.

I remember interviewing for a potential youth pastor position. In the process, I met a big husky football player. I thought that guy would be great with kids. So he came in, and various other staffers interviewed him, including my wife. She even met his wife. Then she strongly suggested, "Don't hire him." I said in reply, "Look, he is a handsome guy. He's played football; he's been in all these training programs for discipleship. He'd be great!" So I hired him and even gave him more money than I should have. I really wanted him.

Six months later, I had a problem. I liked him, but none of the kids liked him. Unfortunately, I had to let him go because it wasn't happening. I've learned the value of inviting other leaders to participate in the staff interviewing process.

This *RATE* comes from one of my best friend John Maxwell's books. It's simple to use and provides helpful information.

R is for Relationships. If potential staff persons do not like people, you should not consider them. If they did not get along with people in previous assignments, they will not get along with people in your church.

A is for Attitude. Give me a person with a great attitude, and I will show you a person who is probably going to do well in ministry. You always want to have a conference with the spouse to check his or her attitude about ministry. I have never had a staff member whose spouse had a bad attitude that did not eventually take them out of ministry.

T is for Talent. Giftedness and talent are significant. What are the unique abilities this prospective staff member brings to ministry? How do his or her talents fit the needs of the church? And be sure to check with others who know the person to be certain that one is as competent in the area of specialization as the prospect thinks himself or herself to be.

E is for Experience. Check out their experience. Try to establish whether they are growing persons and developing professionals in their area of specialization. Some Christian workers have 15 years of experience, which simply means they have only 1 year of experience they repeated 15 times.

SIX KEY ISSUES WHEN HIRING FROM THE OUTSIDE

Since staffers hired from the outside may not fully understand what your church is trying to accomplish, I suggest that you satisfy yourself about six key issues before you invite them to come.

Philosophy of Ministry

Be sure the prospective staff member understands your philosophy of ministry and commits to it. Many potential staffers who have been theologically trained and many Christian workers with years of experience have developed their own philosophy of ministry that may or may not fit with yours. Without agreement at this point, the new staff member will be in perpetual conflict with your vision for ministry.

Ministry Centered

Look for staff persons who are ministry centered, not just looking for a job or position. Look for those who share your church's core values and want to win people for Christ. That means they understand ministry to be a way of life rather than a 9 to 5 profession. And it also means they see eternal dimensions in what the church is doing.

Staff Compatibility

Any staff person you bring from outside must be able to fit in with the present staff. I needed a singles pastor. The person who started our singles ministry was with us for 15 years. So I went recruiting all over the country, looking for the right person. I met a prospect in a Midwestern city and interviewed him three times. I liked him a lot and thought he would be great. I invited him to meet with our personnel committee. I had him meet with the key staff members. In a staff meeting after he left, I said, "Let's talk about him. How do you see him fitting in on the staff? Let's write up all the things we liked about him."

Nobody said anything. So I said again, "Come now, tell me what you liked about him." Nobody said anything. I suspected I was in trouble.

Then I said, "Let's write on the board what you don't like about him." And they immediately suggested about eight things. I said, "That's a no-brainer. He's not coming in." And when I saw those things on the board, the light went on, and I saw he would not fit. I was wrong, and the staff was right. So as you grow your church, it is important that the team fits together.

Master Plan of Staff

Hire only people who fit your master plan. A plan of staffing is a way of fitting the human resources with your vision for your church. What would the staff look like when you put your dream on paper? What would it look like from the inside out? In some ways, you build a staff over years as you design a building. You determine what ministries will work out of that building and design the building around them. It is similar with a master plan of staffing. If this is what my dream church looks like, what kind of staff do I need to make the dream come true?

Successful Ministry Experience

I like people who are over areas they feel some ownership for—a specialized area of ministry they can build, they can dream about. But it's important that when you hire from outside, you are sure you do not have persons inside who have better experience or skills than the person you are considering.

Teachable Spirit and Continual Learner

No leader can teach and develop others who is not a learner himself. Staff members should be shown how to teach each other about ministry. Sometimes that can be done in part of the staff meeting. In the interview process, it is sometimes helpful to ask prospective staff members what magazines and books they have read recently and what seminars they've attended. Their reply will tell you a lot.

THE POSSIBILITIES OF STAFF DEVELOPMENT ARE INCREDIBLE

If ministry is discovering and developing people spiritually, then staff formation and nurture stand at the center of all we do in ministry. Your congregation probably has many Jerry Schmidts and others like him within its network of friends and volunteer workers. Staffers for tomorrow may already stand in your congregation today.

In growing a staff, either from within or without, it is essential that the senior pastor value them and respect them for who they are and for the ministry God has called them to. That is why I have never liked the title "assistant pastor." It suggests somebody who runs around doing what the senior pastor does not want to do. Whether you bring people on staff from within or from without, you want those who are the best at whatever ministries they lead. That means they must be valued for their commitments and achievements too.

Teaming in ministry is like a great 11-person football team. To win, everyone is needed to play various particular positions. No one asks who is the most important player of the 11 men on the field. Is the quarterback more important than the center? How would you like to be a quarterback without a center in front of you? Any coach knows that players at each of those 11 positions are as important as any of the others.

· A church staff team is like that too. An effective staff helps a pastor build a great church when every team member plays his or her position effectively. As I said earlier, you can't beat the right team because in the right environment **T**ogether **E**veryone **A**chieves **M**ore.

◼ *9* ◼

CONSTRUCTIVE WAYS TO PREVENT STAFF CONFLICT
Use Conflict to Unite Your Staff Team

Jim Jackson

Conflict in a church staff is a fact of life, just as conflict occurs anywhere else people live or work. Pastors sometimes cause unnecessary frustrations for themselves by denying that conflict exists in Christian organizations. Of course it exists. Differences of opinion are present wherever two or more people meet.

Conflict for me simply means people process information differently and that they always bring themselves to every situation with their diverse backgrounds, perspectives, ages, experiences, and educations. Conflict is as natural as breathing.

Though I do not go looking for conflict, neither do I work overly hard to avoid it. Conflict, when properly used, provides possibilities for increased understandings and for finding better ways to do ministry. Therefore, every staff member must be helped to understand that conflict does not divide a staff into good and bad guys but unites us as brothers and sisters seeking the best ways to lead the congregation we serve.

Expect conflict, and use it as a challenge rather than a threat. Face realities. The children's director will see things differently than the youth pastor. The business manager will view expenditures from a different perspective than the singles pastor. The custodian will think differently about facilities than the day-care director. The senior pastor may be shocked to discover that he has different priorities than the budget team.

PROBLEMS ASSOCIATED WITH
SERVING ON A CHURCH STAFF

I discussed earlier the advantages of serving on staff. But there are some disadvantages too. The domino effect is the first glaring disadvantage: when something goes wrong in one area of the church, it is likely to create a huge drag on your ministry too.

It is like a well-adjusted family. When something goes wrong with one child, the whole family is negatively affected. A friend likes to remind me that you can only be as happy as your most unhappy child.

In his book *Multiple Church Staff Handbook,* Harold Westing calls these problems staff infections. Using medical terminology makes it sound as if the problems might be contagious but that they might be treatable. Infections also can be prevented and avoided. Those in solo church assignments do not have to face this problem, but they have others.

The second difficulty is that the leader has to let go of some phase of ministry as staff members are added. If you are a generalist pastor, you have been doing it all. But as you develop a staff, trying to do it all creates difficulties. If you do not relinquish the task, you will be doing someone else's work. On the contrary, if you are a specialist, you have to give up ministries you love to do and trust other people to do those things well.

Such a dilemma often happens when one of the staff creates a new ministry as a part of his or her assignment, and the new ministry grows so large that an additional staff member must be hired to lead it. That is difficult for the originator to release, especially when the new staffer does not seem to be doing it the right way.

The third problem is the development of sensitivity issues. How easily they seem to grow! Ego problems sometimes develop when things go well in one area and not so well in other areas. As a result, one staffer feels slighted or jealous of the success of another. Then, too, ego problems grow out of overly close human relations—something like sibling rivalry among children.

The fourth item is division that pops up over issues like perceived inequalities. Sometimes silly things like office furniture or reserved parking places fuel the problems. Sometimes budget differences between ministries or invitations to lunch with the pastor can generate problems. Unfortunately, people often divide up and conquer a weaker person.

On one occasion an associate pastor led a revolution against a midmanager. I was forced to meet with staff groups to let them know I was absolutely committed to the manager. The opposition leader isolated himself and ultimately resigned.

Perhaps ministerial myopia is the most harmful of all staff infections.

Every staff person has spheres of influence among laypeople who get involved when they feel their staff friend is being treated unfairly. In that kind of situation, real problems can develop almost before you realize it. You must move quickly to correct them.

Perhaps ministerial myopia is the most harmful of all staff infections. This malady shows up when staff members see only their ministry. They either overlook the whole or ignore it. This sometimes happens in music departments. There seems to be an unwritten formula: the better people are in their ministry field, the more likely they are to suffer from this myopic condition.

To correct this illness, the senior pastor must continually cast the vision and help everyone see how all the parts of the puzzle fit together.

Regrettably, too many church leaders react to problems rather than proactively manage them. Sometimes clergy persons intentionally ignore an issue until it becomes big and threatening and visible. But why not predetermine a proactive action before the problem appears, since many potential problems are predictable? Such a proactive approach might even prevent some problems from starting. Our challenge is to consider ways to become more proactive in our leadership practices. Our goal is to keep staff problems from starting.

Make Sound Investments at the Beginning of Tenure

Go slow in the hiring process. Among the best ways to keep problems from developing is to anticipate and solve them early, even during the hiring process. Don't oversell the job to attract new staff persons. They have to want to come.

It is important to go slow and act intentionally. It is important to accurately discern the candidates' competency, character, commitment, and experience. If you are overeager in recruiting them, you may never be in a good position to effectively supervise them.

Give New Staff Members a Thorough Orientation

The first three months are critical. If you hire a new person, it is important that you invest time in an orientation process. If you do it right for the first three months, you will avoid many problems downstream. Welcome them and celebrate their coming. Be hospitable and encourage your congregation to be affirming and accepting. Early on, recommunicate the expectations agreed to during the first few conversations.

Even though you already did it when they were hired, go back over the core documents. They are really important. Go over them again. Revisit the job description to make sure the new person totally understands what you and the church expect.

Another strategy to help in the orientation process is to give new staff members a legal pad and send them out for three days to look over the facilities and interview other staffers—all the support personnel, and all the laypeople with whom they will be working.

This strategy helps new staff members get acquainted with people quickly. You will be amazed at what they learn and the questions they ask. With fresh eyes, they see things that you overlook. They ask lots of questions. Your dialogue with them after this experience provides a fruitful time to exchange philosophies of ministry and to discuss improvements of existing ministries.

You can customize other staff orientation processes. Set your creativity and imagination free. For example, if you have a young associate who is not developed spiritually, you need to assign him a mentor. In our church, we have a young associate pastor who is tremendously creative and a seasoned associate who is nearing retirement. When I assigned the young associate pastor to the veteran minister, I said, "I want you to mentor him to take over when you leave." A wonderfully warm relationship developed that enhanced both their ministries.

The next orientation step is to ask new staffers to write down their goals for the first three months. This helps new persons get a quick start on ministry. This helps them clarify the specifics of their assignment based on the interviews they conducted. It is a good way to move dreams to realities.

This process also provides a way for the senior pastor to support the new staff member in front of other members of the team. Then to maximize the benefit of this goal-setting relationship, schedule a weekly meeting with the new staff member for informal evaluation.

When a person joins your staff team, he or she will always have two significant questions: "How am I doing?" and "Is my contribution valuable?" It is up to you to help those you lead see evaluations as positive rather than punitive. The main purpose of evaluation is to encourage new staff members. Make your evaluation accurate and positive.

You especially want to affirm effort, character, creativity, faithfulness, attitude, thoughtfulness, helpfulness, productivity, and improvement.

There is another important reason for evaluation. If in the first three months you see a problem and fail to discuss it, you are sowing seeds that will come up as bad weeds for many years into the future. When you see something that needs correcting, talk about it as early as possible. Be honest and straightforward. Remember, you never motivate people to improve by complimenting them when they know they are not doing a good job. You must be lovingly candid.

In this whole arena of relationship, it is important to be extremely generous with your compliments. Ken Blanchard urges us to "catch people doing something right!" You especially want to affirm effort, character, creativity, faithfulness, attitude, thoughtfulness, helpfulness, productivity, and improvement. I use a little note pad with "attaboy!" printed across the top.

In the first three months of a staffer start-up, I want the new member to stretch strengths, improve his or her weaknesses, and learn to work. For the leader, it is a time to proactively head off potential problems. This process is similar to parenting where you loosen up as the child grows and matures.

Provide Ongoing Supervision

Ongoing supervision is not easy because other staffers are busy. The last thing they have time for is supervision of new people. That means the senior pastor must often provide supervision and mentoring. To give it proper priority, you must genuinely believe the only way to multiply your ministry is through your staff. It is tough, but I am starting to see myself in a new light as a pastor-teacher. In this role, I can impact the whole staff on a rather regular basis. Then group discussions and individual dialogue with me naturally follow. The first thing I do is lead devotional experiences at staff meetings that help the whole staff see the big picture. I try to help them wrestle with the issues I think are before us as a church on themes like "A Winning Team," "The Difference in Servantship and Dictatorship," "The Difference in Leadership and Management," "What Is Our Purpose?" and "The Questions of Accountability."

A second way is to help staff develop their skills. The senior pastor can act as the staff equipper. For example, why not prepare a paper on "How to Make an Oral Presentation." It will help them teach Sunday School lessons and make committee reports. Let's realize many people do not know how to do these things. Other subjects that you might consider teaching are "How to Serve as a Worship Leader," "How to Increase Your Creativity," "How to Memorize Things," "How to Write a Mission Statement," "How to Establish Smart Goals," "How to Stop Procrastinating," "How to Manage Your Time," "How to Have Effective Church Meetings," "How to Give Constructive Feedback," "How to Handle Conflicts," and "How to Enhance Self-Esteem in Those You Equip."

The third way I provide ongoing supervision is to manage by means of 90-day goals. My advice is to never try to evaluate and manage staff on the basis of yearly goals. Of course, they have their annual goals that come out of their job description, but to make goals work, ask them to give you two to four things they are going to accomplish in the next 90 days. For a three-month period, I can remember the goals, and I can discuss them whenever the staffer and I meet. When I pray for a staff member, that is what I pray about. When I stop staffers in the hall, I ask how they are doing with their goals. You can only manage people for 90 days at a time, but with a little effort, you can do that well.

The fourth way I provide ongoing supervision is to hold staff members accountable. Accountability and control are different. If you want to have a creative staff, you do not control them on the front end of a plan, program, or ministry but hold them responsible for results. If you manage them before the fact, you control what they do before they start. Creative people want to be free to try even if they fail. If the church is to prosper, they have to have more successes than failures. I tell them we work in a flat-bottomed boat together, and I am going to give everyone an ice pick. They are free to punch holes anywhere in the boat, but we will all sink if they hit below the waterline.

I want them to be free to try things, to be ambitious, to be effective, or even to fail. Remember, if you have to control a team, you will not have creative people. Responsible accountability usually happens when you manage them by their results.

A fifth way to provide ongoing supervision is what I call a developmental review. In an annual developmental review, you are not trying to reprimand people. Rather, you are trying to help them see where they are in their development and encourage them to do even better. I favor a 360-degree review, which means every staff member is evaluated by people over them, beside them, and under them. Too many evaluations are only top-down and provide only a one-dimensional critique.

Two more realities about evaluation must be considered. The first: people are frightened by them. I am in a 50-year-old church where nobody had ever been evaluated before I arrived. So they were terrified when I announced we were going to do evaluations. But they came out of their evaluation feeling good because we have great people. They felt appreciated and affirmed. The other reality is that pastors are afraid to use evaluations to help people improve. We are afraid the people we are evaluating will feel rejected. It takes courage to evaluate your staff. But it has to be done if you are going to have an effective staff.

Work Hard at Staff Communication

Pastors are communicators, but often they forget to inform their staff members about what is happening. Staff people need to be treated as insiders. If the issues you discuss with them are confidential, be certain to make this clear and hold them to accountability. It is better to trust and communicate than for the pastor to leave the staff out of the loop.

Communication is especially important when changes are being made. Realize that your staff has questions. Anticipate their questions and answer them before they are raised. Some of their questions are: why is the change necessary, how will it affect me and my ministry, what do you expect me to do differently, how will I be measured, what are the tools and the support you are going to give me to assist with the change?

Get Feedback from Staff

If you have a staff, you need to get feedback from them. Every January I ask every staff member and all support personnel to answer a question in writing. I usually give them about two weeks to answer, and I insist they get their response to me. They do not sign their names. Here are questions I have used in the past:

1. What would you suggest that we do differently if we were starting Chapelwood over from scratch?
2. What would you change if you had a magic wand and could change anything about our staff or church?
3. How can we improve team spirit?
4. How can we do more for less?
5. How can we work smarter and not harder?

I always get some great ideas from this process. We take all their responses, collate them, and bring them back to the staff. I give them opportunity to work with the things they bring up and talk about them. Their commitment and creativity will surprise you.

Provide the Best Pay, Benefits, Training, and Atmosphere

It is important to pay people well and reward them for competent service. Once you have good people, it is much easier to hold on to them than to find new ones. Part of keeping them is providing adequate pay packages, training opportunities, and atmosphere. But it also includes the things you do to make people feel appreciated.

THREE AWKWARD STAFF PROBLEMS

In nearly every staff seminar I have led or attended, three tough questions are asked, each of which can contribute to conflict.

Inherited Staff

What do you do with inherited staff? It depends on your polity. Some churches have a rule that when a new pastor comes, everybody submits a letter of resignation. That system has some strengths and some weaknesses. When you inherit good people, you do not want to lose them. But if they are told everybody must submit a letter of resignation, they immediately start looking for another place. Guess who gets hired away from you first? The best people! Guess who is going to be around wanting to continue? The weakest, marginal people.

Automatic resignations are not an option in my denomination. We have a consultation system. Sometimes you need to remind the bishop of which personnel needs to move. My position has always been that since I do not want to move, but if the bishop or superintendent wants me to take another assignment, then we will have to talk regarding staff.

I have never moved when I did not sit down with the staff-parish committee to discuss whether I was the right person for that church and what they wanted to say to me about staff. My experience is that within two years, half the staff will be gone.

I think it is important to help staff members move if they decide to leave. I don't ever want anybody on staff that does not want to be there. I tell them, "If this isn't where you want to be, I want to help you move to a place where you will be happy and useful."

On the flip side, some people need to stay. When I arrived at the church I now serve, I followed a minister who had been there 36 years. One of the associate pastors had been there for all those years with him. I sat down with the associate and took a calculated risk that he could transfer his loyalty to me. My discernment proved to be Spirit-led. That staff person has helped me more than you could believe. So it may be self-destructive to start with an assumption that they all have to go.

The important thing to remember when you are keeping inherited staff is to set the bar of expectation high. They will sort themselves into one of two groups quickly: the whiners and the achievers. If you lower the bar to accommodate the whiners, you will lose your achievers and your right to lead. Keep the expectation bar high, and the whiners will either leave or fall into line.

Staff Changes

How do you make staff changes? Staff changes are always a challenge because they are disruptive to the congregation and other staff members. Start with the assumption that any staff member has at least 100 people in their sphere of influence. If they are really good, they will have many more. Those persons in their sphere of influence can wreak havoc.

If these people want to go, I suggest you help them do it in style. New staffers usually come in about the same way the last person went out. So if you want the new person to be accepted quickly, you should make certain you bless, reward, and deal with all issues the departing staff member leaves.

Here is how it works. If you have a group that feel the person leaving was abused, they are still angry when the next person arrives. They even feel mad that everybody is happy about this person's arrival. Such an attitude by even a few people can make for gross unpleasantries.

To circumvent such a reaction, give the one who is leaving a big reception. Froth about how wonderful he or she is, and give a generous going-away gift. It is important to be generous.

Terminations

What about terminating staff? This is never fun, but sometimes things do not work out. Failing to make the hard and politically unpopular decision to terminate people can produce a cancer in the congregation and the staff.

We live in a contentious and litigation-focused society. That means that pastors have to protect themselves by keeping good records. Hold on to all your development review records. Document everything. When a staff member does something immoral or inappropriate, do not hide it. Make sure the church committee that helps with the supervision of the staff is informed. Do not hesitate to write memos, which the staff members should sign, and keep them in a personnel file. It would not hurt to recruit a labor attorney to serve on your staff supervision committee. If you do terminate a staff member, be careful how you handle the job references you receive concerning him or her.

REVISIT THE KEY ISSUES

To have a productive church staff means multiplying ministry. The best way to deal with conflict is to eliminate its causes at the beginning when a staffer joins your ministry team. Expect some conflict because of the differences of skills, strengths, and perspectives. Keep conflict to a minimum by using well-reasoned core documents, cultivating a team spirit, serving each other as Christ serves you, modeling the church you want your congregation to become, and allowing Christ into the details.

Together you can accomplish amazing achievements for the King of Kings.

COACHING STAFF AND LAY LEADERS FOR GROWTH

How to Shift from Lectures to Experiential Learning

Carl George

Imagine having to make the following tough decision, based on an experience from Dale Galloway, executive editor of this Beeson Leadership Series. The question it asks applies to whatever church role you serve, from senior pastor to lay leader. It involves a family new in the faith, new to the church, and new to the care of a small-group leader.

Back when Dale was pastoring New Hope Community Church, Portland, Oregon, he championed the idea of small groups led by lay pastors and apprentice leaders. He led the church to start hundreds of Tender Loving Care Groups all across the city. Seven days a week, morning through evening, the people of the church met needs in Jesus' name through "one another" pastoral care in those groups.

One of these groups was led by a taxicab driver. On a particular Saturday evening Dale received a call at his home from a member of that group. The group had gathered at the home of a grieving couple who were neighbors of the group leader. They had recently joined the group.

This new couple was in the midst of a crisis. They had reared a child by adoption. She had become estranged from them and had moved to another state. That morning she had committed an atrocious murder. It had become so newsworthy that it was now a network event. Camera crews were lining their property, hounding this dear family who was in the cab driver's small group.

Members of the small group had immediately rushed to their side to give them protection and comfort. From the house they dialed the Galloway home and said, "Pastor, would you like to drop by? Turn on the evening news, and you'll see why." Dale Galloway quickly found the news story on television and headed out the door.

When Dale arrived at the home, a group member welcomed him in. He noticed small-group members already there, bringing in food, covering the phone, attending the doors, and sitting with the couple. He sat down and grieved with them.

After about an hour, the cab driver dismissed him, saying, "Thank you, Pastor, for coming by. You have a lot to do to get ready for tomorrow. We appreciate you coming. Would you lead us in prayer before you go?"

After Dale left, he began thinking about what had just happened. He had been called to a newsworthy trauma to render pastoral care. An hour later, he had been dismissed by a cab driver to go about his other duties. This family in crisis had been cared for as well as—if not better than—if Dale had not even been in town.

"Is this really what I really want?" he asked himself. "Is feeling and being this dispensable to the ministry of this family OK?" Dale was confronted with a decision—among the most difficult decisions—every pastor must face, sooner or later. Most of us might not have the presence of mind to further ask: "Is this nonprofessional kind of care delivery something that God really wants for His people?"

His answer was a resolute *YES.* "This is exactly how God wants the Body of Christ to function. It is working. God is good." With a glad heart, he headed away to get ready for the next day.

Suppose you were one of the people in that true story. How would you feel? Would you want people in your church to know that God is as close as their small group? Do you want them to be confident that they can get significant pastoral help whether the pastor(s) are in town or not? If so, are you willing for your church's pastoral staff to focus their energy on creating a volunteer leadership—hundreds of people like the lay pastor above—who provide nurture and care for the entire membership and beyond?

The Change Begins in Your Head and Heart

Most pastors and lay leaders have to make an enormous mental modification before they can become an effective coach of lay caregivers. They must decide that the most strategic use of pastoral staff is to create a skilled and empowered leadership pool of small groups and individualized ministry. For clergy, the shift is from being pastors to being the creator of other pastors. For lay leaders, it's a shift from doing ministry alone to creating other lay ministers.

The kind of comfort people need and the amount of time they need is such that it must come from volunteers. Otherwise most needs today will become neglected.

For some church leaders, this idea leads to disappointment. They love being caregivers, and they feel a little cheated by the scenario above. They tell themselves, "I was called to love people and teach God's Word, but now I have to spend my time trying to figure out how to be a *maker* of caregivers and to help *others* teach the Word. So everything I get to do happens as a model or teacher or coach. I do not get to do it alone."

Others ask, "Why can't I make a call at the hospital to love somebody, and come home and feel clear and good about it? Instead I feel somewhat guilty that I didn't take a rising leader or two to the hospital with me so I could train them how to do it, with the idea that they could have the privilege of ministry with the next case."

It's not always fun. People's need to receive pastoral care becomes the preeminent focus and not "my" need to give pastoral care. Ministry focuses on meeting the needs of the flock and beyond. The end point is to give up your ambition to be a minister in favor of embracing the vision of ministry for other people. When that is happening, then your calling is being fulfilled.

Learn by Developing an Acquired Taste

You say, "But I have needs too." There is plenty of time for you to meet those needs, but it must occur on the way to getting the Body of Christ functioning as Eph. 4 teaches. The meeting of your personal needs is incidental to the larger task.

If you want to build a congregation that is economically sustainable over the next 20 or 30 years, all leaders must come to the point of realizing they will get their needs met, but it will not be the way they previously thought or expected. You will get to hold people's hands, to counsel, and to have a "presence" ministry. You will teach others. You will receive a great deal of satisfaction, but it needs to be a new form of learned satisfaction.

How? Most pastors or lay leaders will need to acquire a taste for seeing people helped through others, for seeing the credit go to others, knowing that is what we are really called to do, and knowing that it is really OK. This leveraging idea is not natural for about 95 percent of us.

Discover the Clarity of a Football Game

What if ministry had certain rules like football? Football games have scoreboards that post the quarter you are in and how much time you have left. The more sophisticated version tells you who is carrying the ball, how far it is to the goal line, and how many yards you have to make in this next play in order to get permission to continue to hold the ball.

That level of clarity is what most people in ministry only wish for. That is why I think football is so popular. It takes much ambiguity out of what is going on. We know where we want the ball to go. We know who should be carrying the ball.

The clarity of the football game is something you and I only dream of for the church. We love the idea that football coaches and players can give their entire focus to a 3-foot, 3-yard, or 10-yard piece of ground, and then hone in on it.

Coaching is about goals
and helping people get there.

When you can understand your church mission clearly enough that at any one time you know exactly what you have to do in the next 1 minute, 3 minutes, 10 minutes, or one hour in order to achieve the larger game plan, you will have come a long way.

The role of coaching helps you identify your yard marker and strategy for the next play. Good coaching involves far more than delegating, supervising, managing, leading, modeling, or even advising. It may contain all of those things, but it requires something else.

Coaching is about goals and helping people get there. Coaching comes out of the game category with its enormous clarity of win-lose or points within a quarter. Coaching is about performing well within a clarified circumstance. It is about asking, "What is it we are trying to do?" It is about establishing goals, clarifying goals, then achieving goals.

Sometimes, from lay minister to senior pastor, you need to back off and say, "My goal is to survive the next 24 hours by breathing deeply." There are times when if God does not show up, your goose is cooked. In those cases, all you need to do is stay and keep praying.

So your goal is sometimes not about achievement as much as it is about being. My goal is to be so aware of what God is saying that if He says jump, I jump. Or if He does not say anything, I stay put.

Keep Three Questions in Mind When Coaching

Coaches of individuals are guided by two key questions that are different than those asked for coaches of teams. Here is the first question to someone who coaches individuals: What are you trying to do? Ask it over and over again until both you and the person you're coaching begin to hear an answer that makes sense.

The second question for coaches is, "How are you getting in your own way?" The first waves of answers usually turn out to be smokescreens. You will hear, "But you do not understand the difficulties." Or "I can't do it because . . ."

Get to the issue: How are you getting in your own way? Eventually you can help them find the things they can do something about. These matters are within their control, even if it is only their own attitude. Until they define the portion of action for which they are responsible, they are helpless.

You need a third question when you work with coaches of teams. These coaches are guided by high-ground perspectives. Back in the old days when people still fought battles without the advantage of satellites, the commanding generals would frequently take a high-elevation position so they could see the battlefield. The advantage in Christian ministry is that the highest ground perspective is that held by God himself. The problem is that in the middle of the gun smoke and the horse sweat, we lose sight of the fact that God sees clearly the big picture of what is going on down here. It is OK for Him to tell us when to move and not to move.

Thus the question to ask is this: If Jesus were calling the shots here, what would He have us do? The expression "What would Jesus do?" should be more than a devotional exercise.

We Teach as We're Taught

In my own experiments and explorations, I've worked on the ideas of how training that translates into coaching and mentoring behavior actually works. My search has been to find a self-replicable method of training. If we could find or invent such, we could achieve quality training at every level of the church as an organization.

Some of the practices I've been testing in the field (and developing in my next book) have to do with this notion that *you tend to teach in the same manner as you learned.* If you've been taught by lecture, you'll take what you've learned and, when you try to apply it to a new learning situation, will select as your preferred model of training the lecture as you've been lectured to.

In the early stages of the dissemination of knowledge, that's a very common pattern. If people are excited about what they've learned, they take the lecture outlines home, create a seminar environment, and replicate the word track. So the behavior that you proffer with the new knowledge is the old lecture behavior with handouts and word tracks, rather than an embracing of the behaviors that are suggested by the new practices about which you are lecturing.

To Change Behavior, Do So Behaviorally

When it comes to training and preparing coaches, I began to see the same thing. I'd prepare training titled "How to Coach." I'd get coaches together and I'd show them, "Here's how you coach." When I'd visit their church as a consultant, I'd find that they had taken my outlines and turned them into a lecture, a word track about coaching without the "show me" behavioral dimension.

The lectures alone didn't change their behavior. The group leaders would still be coaching as before! Their learning needed to be experiential and behavioral.

Then I began to realize that when Jesus taught His disciples, the bulk of His training was not homiletically organized. Beyond a few sermons, all the rest was done in behavioral settings. He would make observations, coaching and urging people to change their attitude or behavior, in the middle of life's reality.

We've turned the *teaching* method of Jesus, which was on-the-job, into the *lecture* method of Jesus! Jesus did far more to help people learn than to lecture them; He went into life with them.

I began to wonder and explore a new question: what it would be like if we could coach someone and let another coach watch it happen? Then, what if we turned around and let that coach in turn coach someone else? And what if, after watching each other actually coach someone, we take time to talk about how we're doing at it? This would be an action-reflection methodology, somewhat like what we saw Jesus doing.

Shift from "Telling" to "In-Life" Coaching

Once that breakthrough occurred, I realized that many churches have hindered their entire small-group systems by an overreliance on "telling" as the primary teaching method.

Down at the cell group level, where we hope people will be so close to each other as to be aware of each others' needs and lives, we're instructing our group leaders to draw out spiritual-gift-based help for one another. We want the group members to exhort or teach or show mercy or encourage, based on their respective gifts. We want them to try to draw people out in those cell meetings.

But too often, they are conducting meetings when we wish they could be seeing and helping life transformation happen. We know the members actually live life out away from the group, not in a group meeting; the group meeting is only the practice session.

That's where small-group leaders actually serve their members as a life coach. They bring people together to connect in a little meeting, but the small meeting, like the football huddle, is to legitimize the life coaching that needs to go on for the actions they will take "out there"—where the decisions of life are made and ethical challenges faced.

You don't meet nearly as many ethical challenges in the small group as you do on the job, such as when your boss instructs you to lie. You're told to falsify data on a report. You have a chance for greed or compromise to set in. You've got to figure out what to do! How to be an ethical person in an immoral setting? Or do you have to leave that setting? That's where real life is lived! That's why small-group leaders need to be trained as life coaches, which is a much different task than "telling" our people.

When we train the small-group leader, if we lecture, those we train will turn around and lecture others. If we coach them, to help them get their act together, the greater likelihood is that they won't merely "tell truth" to their group.

Rather, they'll provide genuine coaching for them, because we have modeled it in the way we coach them. How our members play the game of life in the real world will improve.

Use the 3-2-1 Approach for On-the-Job Training

It was this notion that led me to develop what I call the 3-2-1 methodology. The idea follows a simple formula: you take three chairs, you schedule two interviews (one after another), and you schedule one talk-it-over time afterward. So you can create an event, during a two-hour block, that trains pastors and leaders in their coaching skills.

For example, you'd say to a coach or coach-in-training to small-group leaders, "Maria, may I work with you on your coaching?" At the appointed time, you sit in one chair, Maria sits in another, and then you bring in two small-group leaders, one at a time, to fill the third chair.

Your first guest is Abby, a small-group leader. You interview her while Maria watches. You use a preset formula. It's a question set for debriefing leaders that has been field-tested (and is available on my web site for free at <www.carlgeorgeonline.org>). Following this question guide, you ask Abby how it's going with her group. You encourage her, pray with her, and send her away. Maria has been watching all this time.

Now you hand the questionnaire to Maria, saying, "Read these questions to the next person who sits in this chair, just as I did with Abby." Maria doesn't even need to have seen the questions before.

Brian comes in. He, too, is a small-group leader. You watch while Maria interviews Brian about his group, encourages him, prays for him, and sends him onward.

By this point about 90 minutes have gone by. Generally it takes 45 minutes to coach someone one-on-one. This in itself has been valuable because you've coached two small-group leaders with the preprinted question set as your paint-by-the-numbers guide.

Maria and you remain in the room (perhaps others have been present as observers). You turn and ask, "Well, what do you think went well?" "What could we do to help these people more effectively?" "When can we do this again?" You use these final 30 minutes to debrief, sharpen your understanding, and put together a plan to do it again. This reflection about coaching practices is the "1" of the 3-2-1 method.

It's in this adoption of a 3-2-1 methodology that I learned how to hand off my coaching skills to another person while at the same time actually helping two people's ministry. Our methodology goes far beyond merely telling them. This is not in-service training; it has become on-the-job training.

What I've been learning is that this method is working. When I finish training a coach, using this method, that coach can immediately train another coach, because the method is so simple. The questions are set. The 3-2-1 formula is set. The quality formula for the coaching process is assured through the debriefing during the last half hour. Anytime I want to touch up on the training process, I bring Maria back in, and we pick up where we left off.

The equipment requirements are minimal: All you need is *three* chairs, *two* interviews, and *one* talk-it-over. We as coaches have a chance to shape each other's behavior and technique through our conversation.

It doesn't matter whether my "pupil coach" is more or less skilled than I am. It's egalitarian. The information about best coaching practices can flow either way. The person I'm training has permission to speak into my practice, because he or she has a chance to observe my practices, so I have a chance to gain from a stronger person.

In many churches, the pastors are less well trained in coaching and in counseling technique than are individuals in their congregation. So we need a methodology that allows a pastor, without loss of face, to be able to bring a more skilled person into his life.

We're dealing with a God who wants to give help and hope to His people. If you will listen as you walk, He will provide you with the resources you need to be of help to people. That's where the church becomes a life-changing place. It's an exciting place and an exciting time to live.